To

_____

From

_____

Date

_____

CLEERE CHERRY REAVES

focus

HOW ONE WORD A WEEK
WILL TRANSFORM YOUR LIFE

DaySpring

LIVE YOUR FAITH

Focus: How One Word a Week Will Transform Your Life
Copyright © Cleere Cherry. All rights reserved.
First Edition, September 2020

Published by:

21154 Highway 16 E
Siloam Springs, AR 72761
dayspring.com

Written by: Cleere Cherry Reaves
Cover Design: Charles Brock

Printed in China
Prime: J2438
ISBN: 978-1-64454-817-2

Contents

Hi, friend!

Can I just begin by telling you how thankful I am that you are holding this devotional book in your hands? Honestly, I wish we were hanging out in person with a cup of coffee in one hand and this devo in the other—maybe someday! But for now, please know I am praying for you and truly believe that God wants to use this book to speak to you in a mighty way.

Here's the deal: I want it to do more than just encourage you. I want it to transform you. I want it to serve as an accountability tool to help you live with new focus.

This book is based off a challenge I accepted last year—a challenge to focus on one word a week, a challenge to shift my thinking from trying to do *everything* perfectly to just getting better at one practice, one week at a time. That's how Jesus works—He meets us in our diligence and delights in us as we stop striving and begin resting in Him. I don't want us to waste another minute not living the abundant life God has called us to, which means that we are going to have to get serious about what God has told us and start applying the Truth. We can do one word a week, no matter how busy life is, amen?

My challenge to you is to read one entry a week, then really focus on that word throughout the week. Write it on the top of your planner, whisper it under your breath as you go about your day, memorize the supporting Scriptures. When you do this, you're sure to find the power of focusing on one word—one practice, one thing God is calling you to do, whether that be rest, peace, diligence, worship, etc. And at the end of every four weeks, you'll find reflective questions, or "Taking Inventory," to help you see how far you've grown by focusing in.

I am praying for you as you *Focus*. I am excited to see how He shows up for you throughout this process. Please know that you are loved and significant, and with Jesus, you can change the world.

Love,
Cleere

Diligent

The soul of the sluggard craves and gets nothing,
while the soul of the diligent is richly supplied.
PROVERBS 13:4 ESV

Diligent. Did you know that the word *diligent* comes from the Latin word *diligere*, which means "to value highly, take delight in"? In English, we often translate this concept to mean "working hard," which is not completely incorrect. The English definition of *diligent* is "careful and serious in your work, or done in a careful and determined way."

But I think we miss something here. Somehow our translation of diligence has lost the connection between diligence and delight. We try to work really hard, get a lot done, and prove that we are capable of handling tasks. But when Jesus speaks about diligence, He attaches it to delight, to care, to love.

Proverbs 4:23 states, "Guard your heart with all diligence, for from it flow springs of life" (BSB). In other words, when we watch our hearts with care, life is brought forth out of our diligence. It is through diligence that we experience abundant life—a life of delight.

What happens when we only give effort in order to cross off a task but disassociate our delight from our effort? We compromise our potential. We can say (and make ourselves actually believe the lie) that care is not required to complete a task; however, the person who does care and delights in that task completes it in a way that displays the character of God. And isn't that the point of our work? That it would produce in us and in others character that imitates the One who made us?

Maybe *that's* why our work feels so hard-pressed and so much like "workkkk" (you know, the way we say it like we are being shot in the foot). We try to do and give and exert energy while separating our heart from it.

But that's not diligence! That's automation—robotic attention without the assertion of care. Care requires our heartstrings, and that is what He is after.

Let's be diligent in what we do today—even in the annoying, mundane, or particularly difficult parts of our work. Let's ask the Lord for diligence in those. For care. For watchful eyes. For steadfast perseverance. We can dislike the task but delight in the One we are doing it for and choose a different perspective. If we set out to collect a paycheck or build an impressive resume, we will remain frustrated and dissatisfied. But if we approach work to become more like Jesus? We really can find meaning and delight in all things.

FOCUS TIP: This week, when you find yourself in a hard situation, whisper the word *diligence* and walk through it—don't run from it. Try to find the meaning behind it and remember Who you are ultimately doing it for.

Let us not lose heart in doing good, for in due time we will reap if we do not grow weary.
GALATIANS 6:9 NASB

Therefore, brothers, be all the more diligent to confirm your calling and election, for if you practice these qualities you will never fall.
II PETER 1:10 ESV

The plans of the diligent lead surely to abundance, but everyone who is hasty comes only to poverty.
PROVERBS 21:5 ESV

Prepare your work outside; get everything ready for yourself in the field, and after that build your house.
PROVERBS 24:27 ESV

▼

Jesus, help me to be diligent; help me steward life well. Amen.

Kindness

*He has showered His kindness on us, along
with all wisdom and understanding.*

EPHESIANS 1:8 NLT

Have you noticed how kindness is a little trendy right now? There are bumper stickers, T-shirts, and all kinds of products that speak to the importance of kindness. We like to pay it forward when we can post about it on social media. We enjoy serving on a mission team where we had already scheduled: "Okay, this week I will be kind and selfless." We don't mind being kind when we feel as though the action or character will be reciprocated.

But how do we feel about kindness when it's not so easy to be kind or when the subject of our attention isn't someone we particularly like? How do we respond to an interruption in our day when it is asking us to forgo our own schedule and answer the need of someone else? It is in these moments that the source of our kindness is tested. Does it stop based on our preference, or are we walking in the same kindness that our heavenly Father extends to us? The kindness of Jesus is the type that ignores one's own opinion or preference, forgets any mishaps, and decides to simply extend a hand regardless. Many times we fear that if we are kind beyond what is deserved, we will not be able to set a standard or prove a point. But what if our standard was grace and kindness?

What would our lives look like if we decided to be out-of-the-box kind this week? If we chose to respond with mercy, to give without expectation of reciprocation, and to walk in a way that lets others know we are not operating on our own accord, we would allow ourselves to be used to bless others.

We would initiate a new way of communicating that stopped focusing on being right and was instead centered on His righteousness.

Think about a time when someone had been unusually kind to you, especially when you were not expecting it. You still remember it, correct? It is often the little moments that matter the most to us; it is the times where someone has taken the time to see us, when their acknowledgment and generosity felt like the hug we did not even know we needed.

Let us be that same hug, deep breath, and extended hand for others.

FOCUS TIP: This week, when you find yourself trying to avoid that certain someone, remember *kindness* and turn around, talk to them, give them your time, and share the love of Christ.

We prove ourselves by our purity, our understanding, our patience, our kindness, by the Holy Spirit within us, and by our sincere love.

II CORINTHIANS 6:6 NLT

*This is what the L*ORD *of Heaven's Armies says: Judge fairly, and show mercy and kindness to one another.*

ZECHARIAH 7:9 NLT

Never let loyalty and kindness leave you! Tie them around your neck as a reminder. Write them deep within your heart.

PROVERBS 3:3 NLT

Since it is through God's kindness, then it is not by their good works. For in that case, God's grace would not be what it really is—free and undeserved.

ROMANS 11:6 NLT

▼

Jesus, in every interaction, help me to be kind. Amen.

Position

He picked up five smooth stones from a stream and put them into his shepherd's bag. Then, armed only with his shepherd's staff and sling, he started across the valley to fight the Philistine.

I SAMUEL 17:40 NLT

When we think about the story of David and Goliath, we tend to think about the theme of courage, right? David was merely a shepherd boy and Goliath was a giant Philistine man. When David went to deliver food to his brothers, who were fighting against the Philistine army, he saw that everyone was afraid of Goliath and had drawn back from the fight. David was a man after God's own heart who truly believed in the power of God within him, so he stepped up to the plate.

While courage is obvious in this story, it is also important to recognize what allowed David to choose courage in the first place. It was David's humility and authority within each position he was given that further put him in place to defeat the Philistine army and be called a hero. What if David had shamed his lowly state compared to his brothers and refused to show up? What if he had become resentful toward his father and never taken food to his brothers, therefore never laying eyes on Goliath?

Many times in our own lives, we are frustrated with the position we are in at the current moment. We don't understand why the dots have not connected sooner for us, why we were given certain gifts and not others, and why God does not elevate us when we feel ready to take the next step. However, if life were based on our own plans, Jesus knows that we would undercut our own potential, settling for whatever position we deemed impressive or glamorous. He knows that, many times, what we think we want is not actually what we *really* want and certainly not what we need. With His tender but firm hand, He guides us down roads of righteousness, allowing our perseverance to be formed and our character to be developed. David killed lions and tigers while protecting his sheep, which made Goliath seem far less intimidating. What if the fire we are walking through now is preparing us for the victory that is up ahead?

He is God. He can connect us with any place and any person at any moment and open any door wide open. However, His ultimate priority is the position of our hearts. Are we seeking Him? Are we striving, or are we resting in His grace? Do we trust Him? The real battle was never against the Philistines; God's desire was for the Israelites to realize that the victory was already theirs because of the power that comes from being positioned in God.

May we be like David—never underestimating our current place and believing that God's power will always position us for what is next.

FOCUS TIP: This week, pay attention to where God has placed you—in your workplace, your family, your community. Think through the many reasons He put you in this exact position. Look at your surroundings. Your position is not an accident.

Therefore, dear friends, since you have been forewarned,
be on your guard so that you may not be carried away by
the error of the lawless and fall from your secure position.

II PETER 3:17 NIV

Behold, I am going to send an angel before you
to guard you along the way and to bring you
into the place which I have prepared.

EXODUS 23:20 NASB

Many are the plans in the mind of a man, but it
is the purpose of the LORD that will stand.

PROVERBS 19:21 ESV

What then shall we say to these things? If
God is for us, who can be against us?

ROMANS 8:31 ESV

Jesus, my position is in You.
That is my security. Amen.

Follow

My children, listen to Me, for all who follow My ways are joyful.
PROVERBS 8:32 NLT

Do you find it strange that the disciples never once asked, "Where are we going?" when Jesus said, "Follow Me"? So often when we read the Bible, we just brush through situations and setups as though they were normal. We read about miracles and think, "Oh yeah, this is the part where Jesus walked on water."

Hello—rewind, please. Did we just say "walk on water"?

And then we read about the different people in Scripture—in particular, the disciples—and we nonchalantly read the text. We read or hear the Bible more like a romantic storybook than a historical recollection of true events. But here's the thing: the disciples had no idea where Jesus was going next. These men were not told ahead of time and therefore not made privy to information about their being disciples. At the time they decided to follow this man *Jesus*, they had no idea that their journeys would be etched in history forever. They did not know they would be famous historical figures.

They simply knew, "Okay, that One, He is it. He is Jesus. He's the One we've been told about! Our rescuer." Since they followed Jesus without knowing what was ahead, how can we not also follow Him?! When Jesus asked them to "come," they didn't request a tour map first. Their direction was uncertain, but they trusted their leader. Their "normal" was interrupted but they believed He was worth it. They were ordinary men who believed that Jesus was who He said He was. They believed that the true risk would be staying behind when they were given the opportunity to partner with their King.

Sometimes we get so caught up in the "how" that we want Jesus to show us the dots before we sign up so we can start connecting them. We want to know more because, somehow, we have convinced ourselves that then we will definitely follow. But the more we walk forward, the more we understand that the uncertainty is actually grace. Unpredictability is His covering. If we saw the dots, we wouldn't believe we are capable of connecting them. If we saw the future, it would feel too risky, too mighty. It would be too much for our shortsighted minds.

But God. It has never been about our ability. Our heavenly Father has always been more captivated with our trust than our talent. He says, "Follow Me" because He wants us to understand that the journey is about exactly that—the journey. As we walk, we talk. As we walk, we witness. As we walk, we worship.

We begin to understand why He is worthy of our trust and stop obsessing over the destination. No longer concerned about our inability or uncertainty, we just grab His hand. And we learn with every step that He is worth the risk.

FOCUS TIP: This week, when you start feeling the weight of the world on your shoulders, think of the word *follow*. You aren't the leader; you aren't in control, but you follow the One who is over it all—and He loves you deeply.

You must not follow the crowd in doing wrong.
When you are called to testify in a dispute, do
not be swayed by the crowd to twist justice.

EXODUS 23:2 NLT

Stay on the path that the LORD your God has commanded
you to follow. Then you will live long and prosperous
lives in the land you are about to enter and occupy.

DEUTERONOMY 5:33 NLT

Lead me in the right path, O LORD, or my enemies will
conquer me. Make Your way plain for me to follow.

PSALM 5:8 NLT

Then He said to the crowd, "If any of you wants to
be My follower, you must give up your own way,
take up your cross daily, and follow Me."

LUKE 9:23 NLT

▼

*Jesus, where You lead,
I choose to follow. Amen.*

▶ taking inventory:

Take a few minutes to reflect upon the last four weeks. How did it go? What is God showing you?

DILIGENT

1. How did focusing on diligence bring you delight?

2. Did asking the Lord for watchful eyes help you to be more diligent?

3. Where did you find it hardest to be diligent? What area or relationship? How has focusing on diligence helped you overcome this situation?

KINDNESS

1. How did focusing on the word *kindness* change your perspective?

2. Did you find that you were more aware of when others showed kindness to you?

3. What would it mean for us to be kind like Jesus all the time?

POSITION

1. How did focusing on position help you match your plans with God's purpose for your life?

2. Were you able to face the Goliaths in your life by stepping into the position in which God has placed you?

3. How did God's power show up for you the week you focused on position?

FOLLOW

1. Why do you think humans have always struggled with being swayed by the crowd?

2. When focusing on the word *follow*, were you able to release full control to God?

3. Did you notice a difference when your priorities, time, and energy were focused on following Him? What was the main difference?

Dear Jesus, thank You for the ways that You show us how diligence and delight are always connected. Help us not to disassociate our hearts from what our hands are doing; we are not merely doers—we are disciples. Show us how to find gratitude and delight in all we do. Thank You for the opportunity to extend kindness to myself and others. Help me to treat others the same way You treat me, always sacrificially showing up far beyond what I deserve.

I am so grateful for Your guidance and Your goodness—I know You are positioning me for a life of righteousness and peace. Help me to trust You with the place I stand, the platform I have, and the people in front of me.

And thank You for the privilege to follow You. Give me courage and trust. You will always lead me with security and peace. In Jesus' name, amen.

Discipline

*A man without self-control is like a city
broken into and left without walls.*

PROVERBS 25:28 ESV

Have you ever had something on your to-do list that you avoided like the plague but once you finally decided to cross it off, it was so much easier than you expected? Maybe once you completed the task, you realized you were actually way more capable than you thought you were before.

Many times we give ourselves too many excuses. We procrastinate, putting things off, claiming that we will do them later once we are "feeling up to it." But this only leaves space for the weeds of doubt and dread to grow. Establishing discipline in our lives allows us to maximize our potential.

Discipline is exactly as it sounds—sometimes hard, sometimes annoying, sometimes frustrating, and sometimes tedious. However, discipline has always been a precursor for righteousness: "Discipline yourself for the purpose of godliness" (I Timothy 4:7 NASB). When we discipline ourselves, we force ourselves to go against our nature. Discipline is the heavy door that leads to the freedom we desire. It feels confusing to think that the life we want is on the other side of denying our *right now*, but that is exactly it. When we live in a disciplined manner, we take on a heavenly perspective, knowing that what is good for us is often not what *feels* good to us.

As we begin to walk the narrow road of a disciplined life, we experience the peace, joy, and love God offers. When we misstep, we receive the grace that He lavishes on us as He reminds our soul of why His way is greater. It is in our pursuit of righteousness that our hearts develop a love for following Him. As the Holy Spirit makes His home in our hearts, He shows us how to tap into the power inside of us as we discipline ourselves in Jesus. Through this process, we come to understand that the risk of going the narrow route is always worth it.

The more our heart, body, mind, and spirit learns how to deny itself, the better we become at choosing righteousness and the more we desire it. Discipline is the passport to a fruitful life; it is the ticket to sitting on the front row of a miracle.

FOCUS TIP: This week, when you make decisions that are pleasing to God—decisions that deny your desire for instant gratification—remember that following Jesus will lead to a life of indescribable peace and overwhelming joy. What could be better than that?

The Spirit God gave us does not make us timid,
but gives us power, love and self-discipline.
II TIMOTHY 1:7 NIV

Whoever heeds discipline shows the way to life, but
whoever ignores correction leads others astray.
PROVERBS 10:17 NIV

No discipline seems pleasant at the time, but painful.
Later on, however, it produces a harvest of righteousness
and peace for those who have been trained by it.
HEBREWS 12:11 NIV

Be hospitable, one who loves what is good, who is
self-controlled, upright, holy and disciplined.
TITUS 1:8 NIV

Jesus, help me to choose discipline.
I want to look like You. Amen.

Worship

How precious is your steadfast love, O God! The children of mankind take refuge in the shadow of your wings.

PSALM 36:7 ESV

Imagine you were given a manual that told you everything about how to live a fruitful life—how to have joy, where to find peace—It has it all. But along with the manual, you have the opportunity to talk to the Author of that manual anytime you want.

You can ask questions. You can present your doubts. You can voice your frustrations. You can lay down your insecurities. You can bring any and all of whatever it is and *He* would bring the manual to life. And, eventually, as you grow older and experience more conversations, you realize that it was in the interaction with the Writer that you began to grasp the manual. You begin to understand His heart.

And though parts may seem redundant or confusing or unnecessary, you remember that He has never included fluff or frivolousness. It is all fruitful. And the hard parts are always worth it.

Isn't this our faith? Our lives? Our Jesus? We have His Word as our manual. But then we have Him! And as we read and we ask and we sit and we do, we get to lean in and say, "Hey, what do You think about this?"

What if we are filling our lives with things to do—things He never asked us to take on?

What if we are walking around with unrealistic expectations—expectations He never placed on us?

What if we keep going, because we will, and then we get twenty years down the road and we finally ask Him: "Hey! Why does my life feel like this? I thought You said *joy*?"

And as He looks at us and grieves the distance we have run, He asks, "*My child, did I even ask you to do all of that? I LOVE you. I've been waiting for you to ask. Sit here. Your life is not a performance to Me. It is your worship. I do not need all you do—I need your attention as you do it. And then I will show you. We will do it together. Oh, how less tired you will be. Together, we will count it all joy.*"

FOCUS TIP: Take a look at your schedule this week and then ask God, "Hey, what do you think of this?" Is He calling you somewhere else? Are you listening? True worship is when you let Him direct your steps.

He is the One you praise; He is your God, who
performed for you those great and awesome
wonders you saw with your own eyes.
DEUTERONOMY 10:21 NIV

Since we are receiving a kingdom that cannot
be shaken, let us be thankful, and so worship
God acceptably with reverence and awe.
HEBREWS 12:28 NIV

You are great and do marvelous deeds; You alone are God.
PSALM 86:10 NIV

Listen and hear my voice; pay attention and hear what I say.
ISAIAH 28:23 NIV

▼

Jesus, my life is Yours.
I worship You. Amen.

Notice

God did this so that they would seek Him and perhaps reach out for Him and find Him, though He is not far from any one of us.
ACTS 17:27 NIV

There are over fifteen lime-green jeeps in my small town. How do I know this? Well, one morning my friend and I saw one and both stated that we had never seen that color of Jeep before. Surely there was not another one in existence for at least another twenty miles, right? However, over the next month, I saw over fifteen Jeeps of this particular lime-green color, all with different bells and whistles, so I knew they were not the same ones. It felt like a prank—that someone specially ordered a parade of this color to hit the streets to put an end to my doubt over its popularity. However, it was never the existence of this color of Jeep in question; it was my awareness of its existence that changed my perspective. It was not until I began looking that I noticed them everywhere!

Our relationship with Jesus is much the same way, but on a much larger scale. Many times we question whether He sees us. We feel like He has forgotten us, or maybe it's just that He thinks our worries or dreams are insignificant. We have a certain time line in our heads or an answer to prayer that we expect, and until He delivers, we feel confused by His plans. But when we begin to take notice of all He is already doing, the ways He has shown up in our past and the intimate manner in which He shows up in our present, our eyes are opened and we see His presence everywhere!

The door of gratitude allows us to enter into a greater perspective, reminding our heart that we know so little but serve a King who created it all.

What if we began to take notice, in the big and small ways, of how God is showing up in our lives and the lives of those around us? In both the blessings that we often feel entitled to, like another sunrise, and in the unexpected places that His fingerprints are seen, He is making Himself known, aka noticed. The "random" encouraging text from a friend, the help on a work project, or the sermon that felt like it was prepared just for us—take note of those moments. The more we look for His hand and His heart, the more we will find them. Jesus never intended to be hidden, but His hope is that we would seek Him and, in doing so, we would realize there is no place that He is not already.

May we be more aware of His kindness and take notice of His great plans for us, creating in us a confidence that He is always taking notice of us.

FOCUS TIP: This week, when you find yourself in the mundane ordinariness of your life, think "notice" and look around you. Then look for the message, person, blessing, or conversation that you may have previously ignored.

O Lord, what are human beings that you should notice them, mere mortals that You should think about them?
PSALM 144:3 NLT

Every good gift and every perfect gift is from above, coming down from the Father of lights, with whom there is no variation or shadow due to change.
JAMES 1:17 ESV

When Jacob awoke from his sleep, he thought, "Surely the Lord is in this place, and I was not aware of it."
GENESIS 28:16 NIV

I am always aware of Your unfailing love, and I have lived according to Your truth.
PSALM 26:3 NLT

▼

Jesus, help me to notice You.
I know You're everywhere. Amen.

Invest

Lay up for yourselves treasures in heaven, where neither moth nor rust destroys and where thieves do not break in and steal.

MATTHEW 6:20 ESV

Imagine you have two homes—one that you are renting for a little while and then another that will be yours forever. Whatever you purchase for the rental will not be able to be kept; once you end your lease, you walk away with nothing you acquired while living there.

The other home is much different—the time, energy, and resources invested into it will not disappear but instead multiply. They will increase beyond measure, be amplified beyond recognition, and grow far past your wildest imagination.

This analogy to our earthly home and heavenly home may sound like too much of a stretch to really be true. However, this is exactly the story of our investment—and yet we wonder where our lack of fulfillment stems from when we pour all our time, energy, and resources into a home we were never meant to make permanent.

Philippians 3:20 tells us this: "We are citizens of heaven, where the Lord Jesus Christ lives. And we are eagerly waiting for Him to return as our Savior" (NLT). In other terms, we are foreigners here, waiting on Jesus. Our souls were meant to crave the comfort that only heaven can offer, that which never wavers and always satisfies. And yet we spend so much of our lives trying to get comfortable in this world, fighting for relevancy and reputation. We are stacking up resources, exhausting all energy, and sacrificing our joy so that we can add to a house we can't even keep. The bragging rights end the moment our lives do, and then what will we say we invested in?

Whether it be showing up to serve others, giving of our finances, disciplining ourselves in prayer, or offering our resources to someone in need, where we choose to invest will determine how much fulfillment we experience. There is a reason we feel this oddly joyful sensation when we give to someone else or when we sacrifice our time without expecting anything in return. It's the exact reason we are here. Foreigners, bringing the Good News to a lost land. Perfection, lasting joy, and peace will never be found in our rental home, no matter how hard we may try. The sooner we remember that we are just passing through, the less attached we will be to things we can't control while we're here. Yearning for heaven, we are meant to invest our time on earth wisely, putting our time, energy, and resources into sharing God's love with others.

FOCUS TIP: Before you make decisions this week, focus on the word *invest* and remember to put your time and energy into the projects that will have an eternal impact.

Here we do not have a lasting city, but we are seeking the city which is to come.
HEBREWS 13:14 NASB

You have been born again, but not to a life that will quickly end. Your new life will last forever because it comes from the eternal, living Word of God.
I PETER 1:23 NLT

One gives freely, yet grows all the richer; another withholds what he should give, and only suffers want. Whoever brings blessing will be enriched, and one who waters will himself be watered.
PROVERBS 11:24–25 ESV

What does it profit a man to gain the whole world and forfeit his soul?
MARK 8:36 ESV

▼

Jesus, here will fade; heaven is forever. Amen.

taking inventory:

DISCIPLINE

1. In what ways has discipline brought good things to your life?

2. How did focusing on discipline transform your relationship with God?

3. Hebrews promises a harvest of righteousness and peace for those who have been trained by discipline. What harvest did you see the week you focused on the word *discipline*?

WORSHIP

1. Did you ask God to guide your feet? Did you change your schedule to make time for His plans instead of your own?

2. Do you agree with this statement: "I do not need all that you do—I need your attention as you do it"?

3. How did you give God more attention the week you focused on worship? How could worship make you less tired or more joyful?

NOTICE

1. What have you noticed about God's work around you recently?

2. As you focused on noticing God, did you find a message, a person, a conversation, or a smile each day that you might have previously ignored? What blessings did you receive by noticing?

3. Have you found your gratitude increasing as you take more notice?

INVEST

1. Think about where you invest your time, finances, energy, talents, and gifts. How much are you investing in your heavenly home?

2. As you focused on making godly investments rather than worldly investments, what change did you make? For example, you spent less time on what? And more time on what?

3. What aspect of your life is God asking you to change? How can you better invest your time?

*Dear Jesus, thank You for loving
me through the discipline of
Your instruction and direction.
It is sure and rooted in love.
I praise You because You are worthy
of it all. Help me to focus on You and go
to You with everything. My life is Yours.
God, You always show up for me
both in big and in little ways.
You created the land and seas and yet
You take notice of me. Help me look
for You, for You are always at work.
And thank You, Jesus, for reminding
me that I am just passing through
here; I was never meant to get
comfortable. Help me invest my
time, energy, and resources into the
only kingdom that never fades.
In Jesus' name, amen.*

Anticipate

I will instruct you and teach you in the way you should go; I will counsel you with my eye upon you.
PSALM 32:8 ESV

The more I experience life, the more I know this to be true: who we become and the story we live has less to do with our planned happenings and more to do with how we react and respond to the unexpected/inconceivable moments of our lives.

Driving home from DC one day, I hit multiple detours and delays. Construction was happening. Tires had gone flat. Wrecks had occurred. People were slowing down just to slow down. With two additional hours tacked on to my trip, I wanted to crawl out of my skin. Every person I passed was equally as frustrated, thinking their obvious hand gestures and facial expressions would somehow make things go faster. And you know what I thought about? Not one of us was in control of what we would face up ahead.

The detour became part of our journey, giving us two choices: (1) beat the steering wheel, make it worse for ourselves, and become frazzled inside; or (2) realize the situation at hand and chill. Stop white-knuckling the steering wheel and release. Forget everything you wish you were doing. And turn on some jams—sing while you wait in anticipation of getting to your destination.

That's how it is with our lives too. Most of what we will face or endure will be unexpected. There will be hiccups and hurdles on the way to discovering and running after our dreams. Curveballs will come, but we get to choose how we will respond.

Will we trust God with every bit of our journey, knowing without a doubt that He has great plans for our lives? Will we look for Him on the detour and realize what He is doing in us rather than think we've been treated unfairly?

Our response to detours and our ability to listen to God after we've made a wrong turn reveals everything we truly believe about His heart. If we know He is good, merciful, abounding in grace, and honest . . . if we believe Him to be all-knowing and ever-present . . . if we have Him placed as the Author of our lives and the perfecter of our faith, then we can forever *anticipate* what is ahead!

Get frustrated. Scream for a hot second. And then move on. Look up. Anticipate what lies ahead. And sing in the wait.

FOCUS TIP: This week, when you hit a traffic jam, when something throws you off track or you receive shocking news, try not to focus on the obstacle at hand, but instead rejoice in *anticipation* of what God is going to do next! He is working out all things for your good. You'll see!

We know that in all things God works for
the good of those who love Him, who have
been called according to His purpose.

ROMANS 8:28 NIV

Trust in the LORD with all your heart, and do not lean on
your own understanding. In all your ways acknowledge
him, and he will make straight your paths.

PROVERBS 3:5–6 ESV

When Pharaoh finally let the people go, God did
not lead them along the main road that runs
through Philistine territory, even though that was
the shortest route to the Promised Land.

EXODUS 13:17 NLT

It is God who works in you, both to will
and to work for his good pleasure.

PHILIPPIANS 2:13 ESV

▼

Jesus, reset and redirect me.
I am looking forward
to what comes next. Amen.

Authority

We destroy arguments and every lofty opinion raised against the knowledge of God, and take every thought captive to obey Christ.

II CORINTHIANS 10:5 ESV

The word *evaluation* feels harsh—it's like a sterile bit of truth smacking you right in the face after a nap that was cut short. It brings to mind thoughts of school testing, midyear employee reviews, and clipboards.

And while it may feel harsh, the truth, is there's nothing wrong with doing a self-evaluation from time to time, to make sure that our thoughts are lining up with God's. The enemy has had way too much say when it comes to how we reflect, view, and dream for our lives. His goal in self-evaluation is always shame; he's terrified of our potential. He doesn't want us to realize the authority that we have in the name of Jesus. He doesn't want us to open our eyes to the ground we can cover when we believe that God is for us and that we never fight a battle without Him. But our Jesus? He is pleading with us to stand in His authority, and to really get it this time—to not let another voice lead to grabbing the shame stick or setting up camp in Why-am-I-like-this Valley or I-wish-this-wasn't-my-life Desert.

The truth? God is eager, hopeful, and absolutely amped about our future. He is not angry at our excuses; rather, He is cupping our face, pleading with us to listen. He is saying: *"Child, don't you see? You have always based your analysis* on your own limitations, but those aren't a concern of Mine. Today, I want you to realize who you are working with. No shame in how we got here; My grace has already covered that. Please let it go. I am filled with hope—pure anticipation—lasting joy about where we are headed, together. You cannot fathom the good that I have planned. You + Me. This will be one for the books. Will you trust Me?"

He knows that when we choose to participate in the gift of life and stop making excuses as to why we can't, we become mountain-movers in a world of doubt.

Our inability? He is able.
Our shortcomings? He has them covered.
Our distractions? He will refocus us.
Our personality? His character never changes.
Our thought life? He will purify us.
Our hearts? He is transforming us.
Our emotions? He is redirecting us to truth.
Our unbelief? His faithfulness will dispel all.

The way to operate in our God-given authority is to reframe our perspective based on Him, not on us. Hand in hand, bringing heaven to earth.

FOCUS TIP: This week, when you start to feel even the slightest tinge of uncertainty, whisper the word "authority" and stand firm in His love.

Behold, I have given you authority to tread on serpents and scorpions, and over all the power of the enemy, and nothing shall hurt you.

LUKE 10:19 ESV

When the Spirit of truth comes, he will guide you into all the truth, for he will not speak on his own authority, but whatever he hears he will speak, and he will declare to you the things that are to come.

JOHN 16:13 ESV

The thief comes only to steal and kill and destroy. I came that they may have life and have it abundantly.

JOHN 10:10 ESV

I tell you, you are Peter, and on this rock I will build my church, and the gates of hell shall not prevail against it.

MATTHEW 16:18 ESV

▼

Jesus, help me to take authority and live with boldness. Amen.

Transformation

*Those who drink the water I give will never be
thirsty again. It becomes a fresh, bubbling spring
within them, giving them eternal life.*

JOHN 4:14 NLT

There once was a little boy whose grandfather asked him to run down the road to the well and fill up his wicker basket. The little boy listened; ran as fast as he could down the long, stony pathway; filled the basket with water; and zoomed back. He arrived sweating and frustrated because every drop of water had disappeared from the basket by the time he returned home. The grandfather sent him down the road again.

Begrudgingly, the boy obeyed and took off again, feeling his feet grow numb as they hit the rocky road. He arrived back—in the same situation. The grandfather wiped away his sweat, expressed his sympathy, and sent the boy one more time. The grandson came back with tears in his eyes, wondering why his grandfather set him up for such a defeating mission.

Seeing his grandson's impatience, discouragement, and exhaustion, the grandfather picked up his grandson and once more wiped his sweaty brow. "Remember how you felt like the Bible wasn't making a difference? Well, we are all like that basket, with His Word as the water. It was your continual returning to the well that helped get the basket clean. Sometimes we don't feel the change, but God is always purifying and transforming us from the inside out."

How often do we feel like the grandson in this story, frustrated that our efforts aren't reaping the reward we were after? We often confuse the point of our journey, thinking that God is more concerned about our fetching water than He is about the state of our hearts, but that is never the case. His top priority is the transformation of our soul, and it is in the journey of fetching the water that this transformation occurs. While Jesus can make all things happen, He allows us to take part in this life because He knows that is the only path to fulfillment and the only way we will quench our thirst.

May we not grow weary in going to the well; may we change our perspective and realize that God is always at work when we are in pursuit of Him. His grace is being made obvious in us; we never waste a step or a moment when the hope of His heart and ours is the transformation within us. Purified from the inside out.

FOCUS TIP: This week, focus on how God is transforming you through every circumstance, every relationship, every detail of your life. Keep your eyes open . . . and get ready to be amazed.

We all, with unveiled face, beholding the glory of the Lord, are being transformed into the same image from one degree of glory to another. For this comes from the Lord who is the Spirit.

II CORINTHIANS 3:18 ESV

And have put on the new self, which is being renewed in knowledge in the image of its Creator.

COLOSSIANS 3:10 NIV

I will give you a new heart, and a new spirit I will put within you. And I will remove the heart of stone from your flesh and give you a heart of flesh.

EZEKIEL 36:26 ESV

I am sure of this, that he who began a good work in you will bring it to completion at the day of Jesus Christ.

PHILIPPIANS 1:6 ESV

Jesus, purify me from the inside out. Amen.

Advance

Solid food is for the mature, for those who have their powers of discernment trained by constant practice to distinguish good from evil.

HEBREWS 5:14 ESV

Remember going to the pool when you were in grade school? Remember how alluring the deep end seemed? It was where all the cool kids hung out! The diving board was at that end, and everyone was doing backflips, and, man, it just looked like so much more fun than standing in the shallow end. Not to mention, anytime there is a rope limiting our access to the other side, we want to cross it, right?

But looking back on it, we know we didn't really have the skill set we needed to enjoy the other side of the pool.

We often operate this way in our spiritual lives too. We say we want deep friendships, but we aren't willing to invest the time or the vulnerability to cultivate those relationships. We claim to desire a strong relationship with the Lord, but the first thing to go in our packed schedule is our quiet time. We pretend we want to serve, but when the deep end requires us to serve someone who is much different than us, we make a swift push toward the ladder to exit. The investment necessary to "swim" in the deep end with Jesus intimidates us or requires too much of us. So, we stay where we are. We keep our floaties on, the goggles firmly pressed onto our face, praying for the lifeguards to whistle and scream,

"Break!" because the shallow end alone makes us tired.

When will we realize that our participation is required if we want to *advance*? When we learn more truth, we are accountable to live it out. When we are freely given the Word of God, we are responsible for reading it. When community is readily offered all around us, we must pursue relationships in order to experience that. We will remain frustrated, intimidated, and continue to experience major FOMO ("fear of missing out") if we stay in the shallow end when our faith was always made to swim in deep waters. We were created to say yes to God in the hard things, to stand firm in situations when the popular thing is to turn away, and to walk through difficulty with the hope of heaven as our guide. Our muscles will stay small and our adventures will be limited if we stay in the shallow end.

Will the deep end require us to abandon some previous habits? Absolutely. But once the floaties come off, we allow God to make our legs strong and the breath of life to guide us into deeper waters.

FOCUS TIP: This week, ask God to help you release everything that is holding you back from advancing, learning, and growing in your faith. Focus on what it might look like to go deeper.

Be doers of the word, and not hearers
only, deceiving yourselves.
JAMES 1:22 ESV

Like newborn babies, you must crave pure spiritual
milk so that you will grow into a full experience of
salvation. Cry out for this nourishment, now that
you have had a taste of the Lord's kindness.
I PETER 2:2–3 NLT

This will continue until we all come to such unity
in our faith and knowledge of God's Son that
we will be mature in the Lord, measuring up to
the full and complete standard of Christ.
EPHESIANS 4:13 NLT

Therefore let us leave the elementary doctrine of Christ
and go on to maturity, not laying again a foundation of
repentance from dead works and of faith toward God.
HEBREWS 6:1 ESV

Jesus, help me to grow.
I want to go deeper. Amen.

▶ taking inventory:

ANTICIPATE

1. What have you learned from the detours in your life?

2. Were you able to focus on anticipating God's next move instead of the roadblocks in front of you?

3. In what ways did you sing during the wait?

AUTHORITY

1. Where do you think you and God are headed together?

2. How did refocusing your heart and mind on Jesus help you to take authority?

3. Is there a specific area of your life that you took back with your God-given authority?

TRANSFORMATION

1. Are you letting God transform your heart and life?

2. Are you experiencing purification from the inside out? How did returning to the well cleanse you?

3. How did you gain confidence in the transformation that God is doing in you?

ADVANCE

1. Did you find any areas in your life where you were choosing to remain in the shallow end? Why?

2. How did focusing on the word *advance* help you grow in your relationship with Christ?

3. What did you do to move toward the deep end?

*Dear Jesus, thank You for being all-knowing,
all-powerful, and all-loving. Help me to
travel with patience and peace, choosing
trust and hope when detours come my way.
I may not like the detours, but I can't wait
to see what You have next for me. I know
You won't let me miss out on my best.
I'm so grateful for the authority that You
have given me—help me to believe it,
choose it, and operate in it. When I feel
defeated by my own limitations and doubts,
refocus my heart and mind on You.
Lord, I know that even when I don't feel
a difference, You are always at work
within me. Help me to be confident in the
transformation that is taking place. You've
transformed my heart in so many ways, Jesus.
Thank You for the invitation to always
grow in maturity with You and in You.
Life in the shallow end is easy and
comfortable—help me to not desire that.
Show me how to advance into deep waters.
I want to grow closer and closer to You.
In Jesus' name, amen.*

Alert

Be on the alert. Stand firm in the faith.
Be men of courage. Be strong.
I CORINTHIANS 16:13 BSB

Fun fact of the day: bats always sleep upside down. Did you know that? It turns out that because their wings do not provide the power to lift them off the ground and their legs are too tiny to give them a running start, they remain upside down and "fall" into flight instead. This is also a tactic to avoid danger, as they position themselves where their predators cannot easily see them—and if they are seen, their position allows for immediate movement.

How often do we operate in a way that anticipates danger? Scripture tells us time and time again that our enemy is out to get us. God's goal was never to instill fear into us; rather, it was to prepare us for what He knows we will face. Unfortunately, too many times we find ourselves surprised by opposition, reacting in fear and doing our best to escape danger without positioning ourselves for peace. We manipulate situations, trying to add "more" so that maybe our stuff will cover up our mess, or we quit and call it defeat. *Maybe I just wasn't made to fly*, we think.

But what if we lived as if we believed His Word to be true? It tells us to be sober-minded and alert. How do we do that? By keeping our minds renewed with truth and our eyes open to the world around us. His Word tells us to be honest about sins and our shortcomings, allowing us to live in the light. This allows us to live in spacious places, as our vulnerability paves the way for honesty and freedom. His Word also reminds us to equip ourselves with the armor of God—the sword of the Spirit, the helmet of salvation, the breastplate of righteousness, the sandals of peace, the shield of faith, and the belt of truth—and to secure it all in the power of prayer (Ephesians 6:10–18). We cannot live as though we do not know what is ahead. We cannot wait to fill up at the well when our cup is empty.

Now is the time to ready ourselves for battle. Now is the time to secure our foundation and read the Word. Now is the time to position ourselves and assure our heart of Who walks with us so that when the valley does come, we will eagerly anticipate His faithfulness.

FOCUS TIP: Think of the word "alert" this week when you find yourself fearful or anxious. And whisper this Scripture: "God has not given us a spirit of fear, but of power and of love and of a sound mind" (II Timothy 1:7 NKJV).

Beloved, do not be surprised at the fiery trial
when it comes upon you to test you, as though
something strange were happening to you.
I PETER 4:12 ESV

The Helper, the Holy Spirit, whom the Father will send
in my name, he will teach you all things and bring to
your remembrance all that I have said to you.
JOHN 14:26 ESV

I have said these things to you, that in me you may
have peace. In the world you will have tribulation.
But take heart; I have overcome the world.
JOHN 16:33 ESV

The name of the Lord is a strong tower; the
righteous man runs into it and is safe.
PROVERBS 18:10 ESV

▼

*Jesus, keep me alert;
ready my spirit. Amen.*

Choose

He must increase; I must decrease.

JOHN 3:30 BSB

I remember mornings in elementary school when the overhead speaker blared, "Have a great day! The choice is yours." As cheesy as it sounded, and as much as we rolled our eyes at the time, we can remember the impact, right? Those four little words, "The choice is yours," packed arguably the most powerful punch placed in our circle of control—that *we* chose how we spoke, acted, and responded each and every moment of our day.

We always have a choice. It's the freedom of the gospel, the authority of our identity and the grace we've been afforded—we get to choose what favors Jesus. Sometimes we get caught up in justifying our actions by logic or cultural norm; however, in that, we forget that Jesus did not seek to make sense; He came to save a watching world. He came to change it, to breathe life into it, and to show a new way, a better way.

In our culture, we tend to negate our own authority in an attempt to earn it before walking in it, or we delay making a choice but do not realize that our delay *is* the choice. Every moment, we are either becoming more like Jesus or less like Jesus.

How incredible is that? Because He lives in us, we have authority over what we decide and how we operate! We are able to experience a setback and still believe in victory. We are able to feel intense emotions in a moment but make a decision based on truth. We are able to release what is not ours to carry and give it to Him instead. We are able to abandon the expectations and standards of the world and decide to live to please our Maker. It really is possible.

Is there a relationship, circumstance, or perspective where you are choosing what is comfortable over what is Christlike?

Maybe a little more kindness, less apathy? More courage, less fear?

More grace, less judgment? More patience, less frustration? More gratitude, less entitlement? More confidence, less insecurity? More delight, less dread?

More generosity, less selfishness? More peace, less worry?

More humility, less pride? More focus, less distraction?

It is always more of Jesus that changes the world. It is never because we are great or that we improve; it is because we surrendered and He saves. May we commit to choosing more of Him.

FOCUS TIP: This week, focus on choosing His ways over yours. When a decision needs to be made, remind yourself that you have a choice and then *choose* Him—every time. No matter how appealing the other road may appear, His way is always going to win.

Today I have given you the choice between life and death, between blessings and curses. Now I call on heaven and earth to witness the choice you make. Oh, that you would choose life, so that you and your descendants might live!

DEUTERONOMY 30:19 NLT

My feet have closely followed His steps; I have kept to His way without turning aside.

JOB 23:11 NIV

You make known to me the path of life; you will fill me with joy in Your presence, with eternal pleasures at Your right hand.

PSALM 16:11 NIV

Enter through the narrow gate. For wide is the gate and broad is the road that leads to destruction, and many enter through it.

MATTHEW 7:13 NIV

▼

Jesus, more of You, less of me. Amen.

Forgiveness

*Good sense makes one slow to anger, and it
is his glory to overlook an offense.*

PROVERBS 19:11 ESV

If there was a literal roadblock in the middle of your driveway, would you move it out of the way before attempting to drive anywhere? Or would you choose to tear up the yard by avoiding it or go ahead and hit it, damaging your car instead? It seems like the silliest question, and yet this is often how we handle offenses in our lives. An offense is like a roadblock; we are the ones who decide whether it remains, because we are the ones who placed it there from the start. Our feelings were hurt or our pride was bruised, and the offense feels justified.

However, the problem with offense is that it most affects the one who is offended. Many times, everyone else keeps backing out of their own driveway, moving on with life, while the offended are left stagnant, frustrated, and prideful. This doesn't mean that the other person was necessarily in the right, but that is the issue with offense—we make it about being right or proving a point. If we think about it, how many times was Jesus betrayed, forgotten, and rejected throughout Scripture? How would Scripture look differently if He had taken offense to the words and actions of those around Him instead of basing His thoughts, actions, and hope on the foundation of His heavenly Father? Instead, Jesus took the cross. He covered all our offenses, allowing us to live lives of promise and peace until we become perfect with Him.

How would our own lives look differently if we made a concerted effort to let go of our offenses and forgive freely? We would be able to run hard after Jesus and trust Him to sort out any infraction or bitterness we may feel along the way. When we choose to focus on the grace that we have been offered, our hearts are more apt to offer grace to others. Since we know that injustice and sin will always be a part of this world, we also know that offense will always be an option. But that is the beauty: we get to choose. We have Christ, and we can decide to forgive those who trespass against us (just as He forgives us for our trespasses against Him). Our effectiveness is not made possible in proving a point but in pointing to Jesus. We will always benefit from honoring God over our feelings.

This week, let's look for opportunities to forgive rather than opportunities to be offended. What a game changer that will be!

FOCUS TIP: As you focus on *forgiveness* this week, search your heart for any past hurts you are still holding onto, and let go of them. Lean on God to help you. Also this week, when you feel yourself starting to hold onto feelings of resentment, focus on the word *forgiveness*, recite the activating Scriptures, and don't allow the roadblock of offense on your driveway.

Peter came to him and asked, "Lord, how often should I forgive someone who sins against me? Seven times?" "No, not seven times," Jesus replied, "but seventy times seven!"

MATTHEW 18:21–22 NLT

With all humility and gentleness, with patience, bearing with one another in love, eager to maintain the unity of the Spirit in the bond of peace.

EPHESIANS 4:2–3 ESV

When he was reviled, he did not revile in return; when he suffered, he did not threaten, but continued entrusting himself to him who judges justly.

1 PETER 2:23 ESV

Brothers, if anyone is caught in any transgression, you who are spiritual should restore him in a spirit of gentleness. Keep watch on yourself, lest you too be tempted. Bear one another's burdens, and so fulfill the law of Christ. For if anyone thinks he is something, when he is nothing, he deceives himself.

GALATIANS 6:1–3 ESV

▼

Jesus, I let go of all my offenses and pick up Your grace instead. Amen.

Rhythm

Learn the unforced rhythms of grace. I won't lay anything heavy or ill-fitting on you. Keep company with me and you'll learn to live freely and lightly.
MATTHEW 11:30 THE MESSAGE

What sounds more daunting: setting the goal to run a marathon or sticking to the rhythm of running an increased amount every week? What about the goal of reading twenty books in a year versus setting the rhythm of reading for thirty minutes before bed every night?

We often set these lofty goals but do not put in place the necessary rhythms to actually follow through with them. Or the goals we desire to achieve feel unrealistic for someone like us. The marathon feels like a joke for the non-runner, and the reading goal seems impossible for the distracted television watcher. However, maybe if we thought about these things in a less competitive, shortsighted way, rather in a more healthy, long-term manner, we would, take a different approach.

All throughout Scripture, it is obvious that Jesus had a different rhythm. He never lived hurried, yet He was the most effective person to ever grace the planet. It is obvious that despite His heavy emphasis on community, He knew that the only way He could truly hear the voice of His Father was in solitude, as He often withdrew to lonely places and prayed (Luke 5:16). The rhythm of Jesus was always in response to the priority of the One who was leading Him. He is our perfect example.

While He was a visionary with eternity in mind, He never let the needs of those in front of Him become unwelcome interruptions. His rhythm was always adaptable to where His Father pointed.

Whether it be our workplace goals, fitness regimen, schedule changes, or personal hopes for our lives, it will be in our new rhythms that we create the necessary parameters to not just succeed but to soar. Goals often feel like mirages in the distance that don't provide incentive to run after, while rhythms create cadences in our soul that reminds us every single day of the power of improvement. Setting a rhythm embraces the fluidity of life, knowing that we often won't get it right or perfect but we will show up. It also enforces a structure that will help us flourish and grow. When we bring our imperfect selves to the feet of Jesus through the discipline of rhythm, we allow His perfection to shine through us.

FOCUS TIP: This week, when focusing on *rhythm*, ask God to help you set the perfect cadence—one that will give you peace and abundance.

*The one who says he remains in Him
should walk just as He walked.*

I JOHN 2:6 CSB

*I say then, walk by the Spirit and you will certainly
not carry out the desire of the flesh.*

GALATIANS 5:16 CSB

*So it's paramount that you keep the commandments
of GOD, your God, walk down the roads He
shows you and reverently respect Him.*

DEUTERONOMY 8:6 THE MESSAGE

*These are the records of the generations of
Noah. Noah was a righteous man, blameless
in his time; Noah walked with God.*

GENESIS 6:9 NASB

▼

*Jesus, set my rhythm;
help me to follow. Amen.*

▶ taking inventory:

ALERT

1. How did reading the Word help you prepare for opposition and the unexpected?

2. Where did you need to open your eyes?

3. The armor of God equips us with the Spirit, salvation, righteousness, peace, faith, truth, and prayer. Did you armor up? How did it feel?

CHOOSE

1. What did you choose to focus on? Less or more of what?

2. How did choosing more of Jesus make other choices easier?

3. What are the best choices you have made in the last year?

FORGIVENESS

1. What do you think it means to "bear with one another in love"? Has anyone ever "restored" you in a "spirit of gentleness"?

2. Why is seven times not often enough to forgive a transgression? Why would Jesus say that we should forgive seventy times seven?

3. What obstacles did you remove from your "driveway"?

RHYTHM

1. How would you describe your rhythm? What adjustments did you make?

2. Have you seen the negative effects of living in a hurry?

3. How are you balancing the needs for community and solitude in your life?

*Dear Jesus, thank You for the way You
prepare my heart for what is ahead.
Help my mind to be alert and my feet
ready for opposition and the unexpected;
may I respond rather than react.
Thank You for the freedom You have given
me, that I get to choose how I live—what
a gift that is! Help me to choose wisely,
always allowing for more of You and
less of me. I want to participate in Your
miracles by pursuing more of You.
Jesus, You are the ultimate example of
grace. I choose to trust You as I exchange my
offense and bitterness for strength and peace.
Thank You for allowing me to walk in
step with You. Show me how to set helpful
rhythms for my life rather than unrealistic
goals. Abiding in You is always the goal.
In Jesus' name, amen.*

Seek

For everything there is a season, a time
for every activity under heaven.
ECCLESIASTES 3:1 NLT

We have glass balls and we have rubber balls, and we are continually balancing and deciding which ones can be dropped. Confused? Let me explain.

In our lives, we have different priorities that we all must tend to, and with every season, they change. During some phases of our lives, certain things become priorities—glass balls—and then in due time their importance lessens—rubber balls. There are other aspects of our lives that will forever remain priorities, such as our relationship with Jesus, our family, and our marriage.

However, most things in our lives are not so clear; they are fluid with each season, and we must become okay with switching from glass balls to rubber balls. For example, let's say you're engaged and planning a wedding: preparing for the big day becomes a glass ball. Or you're in medical school, working on getting a specialized degree: studying becomes a glass ball that you can't afford to drop. You may be working through some heart issues that are affecting your life: counseling becomes a glass ball. Depending on what we are walking through determines what priorities are glass.

How do we know what to consider a rubber ball or a glass

ball in our lives? Stillness with the Father. Through *seeking* what Jesus wants for our lives, we are able to release some of the pressure to keep all the glass balls afloat and surrender what is not ours to hold. In our prioritizing of Jesus, we learn to correctly prioritize everything else, understanding that if everything in life is a priority, nothing is. What is most important to us? What areas of our lives are we specifically called to in this moment that will have an eternal impact in His kingdom? As we *seek* Jesus and His promises, we receive a true peace about what He asks us to release and what He commands us to hold.

If we continue to try to be everything to everyone, we will not be the person we need to be to those who need us most. May we be okay with letting the distractions be rubber balls, not feeling the pressure to keep them afloat. And may we give our attention and love to His best for us, realizing that if we *seek* God and ask Him to reveal which balls are glass and which are rubber, we will find that He will set us on the right path. When He does, the juggling will feel almost effortless because He will give us everything we need to accomplish His will for our lives.

FOCUS TIP: This week, remember to *seek* God when you are prioritizing your schedule. Ask Him: is this a glass ball or a rubber ball? And then listen and go to His Word for your answer. He longs to guide your steps.

But seek first the kingdom of God and his righteousness,
and all these things will be added to you.
MATTHEW 6:33 ESV

So whether we are at home or away, we
make it our aim to please him.
II CORINTHIANS 5:9 ESV

The Lord said to her, "My dear Martha, you are
worried and upset over all these details! There is
only one thing worth being concerned about.
Mary has discovered it, and it will not
be taken away from her.
LUKE 10:41-42 NLT

Be very careful, then, how you live—
not as unwise but as wise.
EPHESIANS 5:15 NIV

*Jesus, help me to seek
You in all I do. Amen.*

Arrive

He will command His angels concerning
you to guard you in all your ways.

PSALM 91:11 NIV

If someone asked you, "How would you describe your-self?" what would you say? Would the answer easily flow, or would you have to think about it for a little while, con-templating what is true and what is not? When it comes to self-evaluation, we tend to be extremely hard on ourselves. I think this is because we are basing our thoughts on two different people: our idealized self and our actual self. We tend to assess ourselves with an impossible gauge, always comparing where we are to where we wish we were, setting a series of unrealistic expectations we will never be able to meet.

This reality creates tension that makes us feel as though we are never truly progressing. We become consumed with the destination, and all we want to do is arrive. We break our backs attempting to attain perfection this side of heaven, which we all know is not within our reach. What if we began to take this word *arrive* and see it in a new light—one that reminds us of how we have already arrived in the exact space Jesus needs us to be. Our weaknesses are His invita-tion to become strong in us. It is in these moments where we must release and trust, that true intimacy grows. Resting in where we are, giving our best, and surrendering the rest to

Jesus would allow us to take the pressure off our own shoulders as we learn to operate on kingdom time.

Where must we arrive? At His feet. That is the only destination that we should concern ourselves with, knowing and believing that He will instruct and lead as He sees fit. We were not given the gift of this life to impress others or race to the finish line as we create robust resumes; we were created to thrive in our brokenness as our heavenly Father infuses His power into every fiber of our being.

Open His Word and let His truth be the standard for your life. Resume your authority as a child of God and choose to practice joy in every step of the journey. Remember that you are not behind, because God is always on time. Remind your soul that you are not aimless, because God uses everything for our good and His glory.

Let's release perfection and pursue excellence until we arrive at our permanent home.

FOCUS TIP: Every time you start to think about being behind or feel defeated this week, think of the word *arrive* and be comforted by the fact that you are exactly where God wants you right now, in the moment, in this place, in this world.

Your word is a lamp for my feet, a light on my path.
PSALM 119:105 NIV

Then they said to him, "Please inquire of God to learn whether our journey will be successful." The priest answered them, "Go in peace. Your journey has the Lord's approval."
JUDGES 18:5–6 NIV

There is an appointed time for everything. And there is a time for every event under heaven.
ECCLESIASTES 3:1 NASB

He knows the way that I take; when He has tested me, I will come forth as gold.
JOB 23:10 NIV

▼

Jesus, I am on time because You are on time. Amen.

Timing

Do not overlook this one fact, beloved, that with the Lord one day is as a thousand years, and a thousand years as one day.

II PETER 3:8 ESV

Have you noticed how when you go on a walk with someone, you're forced to either slow down or speed up? Getting in sync with their rhythm takes some effort and intentionality. And staying there? It requires even more.

You may forgo some speed for the sake of conversation and togetherness. Or you may have to suck a little wind if you're used to a stroll. But eventually, you get it. Your steps begin to partner with each other and you find that balance. Your heart rate adjusts to whatever speed and then. . .

A hill. A twist. A turn.

You had just gotten it down pat when the course changed it up.

A little frustrated, a little unnerved by the uncertainty ahead, you find yourself wanting to get back to that peaceful grind.

And you do. But you also realize that in these moments of transition and terrain change, you learned something new. Your breath may have fallen shallow for a bit, but it regained its depth. Your feet learned how to pivot. Your eyes gained the discipline of staying fixed ahead to prevent your feet from slipping. And your hands? They have to keep swinging, matching the speed of your body, so there's no way they can hold on to their past rhythm or their old behaviors.

The walk. The journey. The continual, daily learning curve. The process. The blessing of taking each step, one by one, being reminded that we are continually being refined. Our joy is not in our arrival but in our walk with Him.

And we can trust Him. His nudges inch us closer to fulfillment. His timing is perfect. He isn't too fast and He isn't too slow. Well aware of the world's time line, we can confidently take each step closer to the One who made the world. He knows. He knows what we've walked through, how tired our feet feel now, and what bends are in front of us. We don't have to try to run up ahead for fear that we have forgotten something behind; He can get us to the next place with what we have in this moment.

FOCUS TIP: This week, as you start to ramp up and go, go, go . . . remember *timing*, and then take a deep breath and ask God to help you go at His tempo.

The Lord is not slow to fulfill his promise as some count slowness, but is patient toward you, not wishing that any should perish, but that all should reach repentance.
II PETER 3:9 ESV

Wait for the Lord; be strong, and let your heart take courage; wait for the Lord!
PSALM 27:14 ESV

For everything there is a season, and a time for every matter under heaven.
ECCLESIASTES 3:1 ESV

For still the vision awaits its appointed time; it hastens to the end—it will not lie. If it seems slow, wait for it; it will surely come; it will not delay.
HABAKKUK 2:3 ESV

▼

*Jesus, walking with You.
Every step, perfect timing. Amen.*

Clarity

"Martha, Martha," the Lord answered, "you are worried
and upset about many things, but few things are
needed — or indeed only one. Mary has chosen what is
better, and it will not be taken away from her."

LUKE 10:41–42 NIV

When we think about things that distract us from what God has for us, we usually assume those things are inherently bad, right? Choices we make that don't line up with Scripture, strongholds and addictions that continually idolize things of this world, and the concept of sin in general.

But when *good* things distract us from what is best for our lives—what then?

The story of Mary and Martha in Luke 10 gives us a great picture of what happens in our lives when we let good things get in the way. Jesus and His disciples were walking through the village and Martha invited them into her home for dinner, where Mary was also residing. While Jesus was in the living room, Martha spent all her time in the kitchen preparing things for her guests while Mary sat at the feet of Jesus as He taught those listening.

From the outside looking in, it is easy to shame Martha for not following after Mary and soaking in every waking moment with Jesus, the One they claimed to follow! However, many times our lives resemble Martha's.

We know Jesus wants to be with us, that He is

speaking—and we know it is important, but we feel pressed by what is right in front of us. The to-do list feels too long to put aside, and we prioritize the preparation for the future over sitting with the only One who controls our future. The enemy does not just use the evil to distract us; he likes to consume us with what is immediate rather than what is important. However, Jesus never asks us to spend time with Him and then puts us in a position where we are too late for what is best for us. He always maximizes our time, replenishes our strength, and gives us *clarity* we did not have beforehand.

Luke 10:42 ends the story of Martha and Mary with Jesus telling Martha, "Mary has chosen what is better, and it will not be taken away from her" (NIV). When we prioritize Jesus, He protects us on all sides and preserves our life. When we give ourselves to what is better, He gives us His best.

Let's take the time to think about what may be keeping us from God's best and be adamant about doing something about it. Let's leave the kitchen and the comfort of our normal, "good" lives and let's sit at the feet of Jesus and simply ask for *clarity*. What might He be saying to us?

FOCUS TIP: God is never surprised. He knows exactly what you are facing and what your future holds. So instead of guessing what your next steps should be, ask the One who can clear things up for you. When you find yourself confused this week, whisper the word *clarity* and ask Him to open your eyes to the bigger picture. And get ready to be amazed!

You shall not make for yourself an image in the form of anything in heaven above or on the earth beneath or in the waters below.

DEUTERONOMY 5:8 NIV

I am saying this for your benefit, not to place restrictions on you. I want you to do whatever will help you serve the Lord best, with as few distractions as possible.

I CORINTHIANS 7:35 NLT

Do not love this world nor the things it offers you, for when you love the world, you do not have the love of the Father in you.

I JOHN 2:15 NLT

For am I now seeking the approval of man, or of God? Or am I trying to please man? If I were still trying to please man, I would not be a servant of Christ.

GALATIANS 1:10 ESV

Jesus, give me clarity.
I want to see through Your eyes. Amen.

▶ taking inventory:

SEEK

1. What glass balls were you holding?

2. What did you drop to keep the glass balls from crashing?

3. Did you experience the freedom of dropping certain rubber balls that were no longer a priority to you?

ARRIVE

1. As you focused on the word *arrive*, what messages did you receive?

2. How is God using your life right now for your good and His glory?

3. Do you feel as though your current journey has the Lord's approval? If not, where is your anxiety stemming from?

TIMING

1. Did you sense a link between waiting for the Lord and letting your heart take courage?

2. When has God shown you His perfect timing? Have you experienced the blessing of unanswered prayers?

3. Was there a specific situation or circumstance in which you had a hard time trusting God's timing? Did you surrender it?

CLARITY

1. Did God open your eyes to see things differently this week?

2. How did pursuing His best for you change your life?

3. What most easily distracts you from spending time with Jesus, even if, like Martha, it's something good?

Dear Jesus, thank You for being King over my time, energy, and resources. Will You help me let go of what isn't mine in this season and trust that You have my best in mind? All is Yours anyway.

In Your gentleness, I ask You to keep reminding my heart that I am not behind, defeated, or aimless. When I begin to dwell on what I lack or where I wish I was, re-center my focus to Your truth. The process is the point and perfection only exists in You. Thank You, Jesus, for helping me keep the pace of my life in step with You. Help me to not live hurried, zoning in on my desires and becoming numb to Your nudges. Step by step, let us walk together, for I know that Your timing is perfect.

I am in awe of You, Jesus. Thank You for giving me the privilege of sitting at Your feet, resting on Your shoulders, and simply remaining in Your presence. Will You give me clarity so that I know, without a doubt, what You want me to let go of and what You want me to pursue? You are gracious and generous with all You give. In Jesus' name, amen.

Little

*One who is faithful in a very little is also faithful in much, and
one who is dishonest in a very little is also dishonest in much.*

LUKE 16:10 ESV

Many times, when we think about what we want to do in this life and the legacy we want to leave, we imagine mighty, grandiose things. We think the bigger and more impressive the task, the richer our legacy will be. Our desire to achieve great things, to make Jesus proud, or to embrace all that life has to offer are not bad things in the slightest; however, sometimes seeing only the bigger picture makes us feel paralyzed by possibility. We see the much that can and needs to be done but we wonder how to begin. We realize the urgency of doing something, but is what we have to offer enough?

When we take the time to sit down and ask for clarity about what is next, the Lord often reveals just the next step or decision. Many times, before we even pray, we know what that is. But it's not just that decision we were praying about; we want more of the plan or outcome revealed before we move forward. In our self-righteousness, we think that if we truly took that one small step, it would not be enough to get us where we hope to go, right?

We undermine the "big" that our God can do with our *little* step, so we clamor and reach for more before going forward. In these moments, what if God is merely looking for our faith in His plan and our belief in His power? It has never been about whether we are capable; it has always been about whether we believe He is *able*.

Step by step, every mountain is climbed. Page by page, every book is written. Mile by mile, every marathon is run. The *little* is never actually little when it's put in the Potter's hands. Whether it be taking an exercise class we've been scared to do, having that tough conversation we've been avoiding, or starting to volunteer one day a month at the senior citizen center—we must decide to show up faithfully in the little spaces. It is not up to us to decide how God will multiply, but how can He work if we refuse to show up for the smallest things?

Do we trust God? That is the honest question. Do we believe that the God of the Bible who multiplied two fish and five loaves of bread is the same God who reigns over our lives today? If so, then shouldn't we be counting on His amazing ways to show up in our lives? May we give our little and our best so that He can make it big and do the rest.

FOCUS TIP: As you approach God with your *little* this week, know that your small steps of faith are so important to Him. And then be on the lookout for God to turn your *littles* into huge events.

[The mustard seed] is the smallest of all seeds, but when it has grown it is larger than all the garden plants and becomes a tree, so that the birds of the air come and make nests in its branches.

MATTHEW 13:32 ESV

His master said to him, "Well done, good and faithful servant. You have been faithful over a little; I will set you over much. Enter into the joy of your master."

MATTHEW 25:21 ESV

There is a boy here who has five barley loaves and two fish, but what are they for so many?

JOHN 6:9 ESV

And whatever you do, in word or deed, do everything in the name of the Lord Jesus, giving thanks to God the Father through him.

COLOSSIANS 3:17 ESV

▼

*Jesus, the little I give,
much You can do. Amen.*

Honesty

Dear children, let us not love with words or
speech but with actions and in truth.

I JOHN 3:18 NIV

I still remember walking into my parents' room and feeling their eyes on me, sensing their disappointment before I even opened my mouth. My hat hiding my eyes as I peered down at my feet, I was dreading this conversation. How was it possible that I had gotten a third speeding ticket within a matter of twelve months? It was no longer about forgiveness and NASCAR jokes; I had received more than enough warnings to slow down and be more aware, yet here I was. I had written down my thoughts on note cards (because, yes, my nerves were that high), and I shared every detail. At that point, what did I have to lose?

Much to my surprise, my parents walked over, lifted my hat off my head, and said, "You are in trouble, but thank you for being honest with us. That is all we ask." I knew I would be riding a Razor scooter for a solid six months, but their response shocked and disarmed me in the same breath. I knew they meant it—honesty is what they always asked of me. They could handle mistakes and broken pieces—together we could work on putting anything back together. But if I refused to tell the truth, how could they help me rebuild?

Honesty is sometimes the last thing we want to practice and therefore the first thing we must. Honesty turns our heart back to Jesus. It provides the pathway to relief that can only be found through the act of repentance. It reminds our soul that even when our imperfection is revealed, His perfection can sustain. It is in the hard but honest moments that Jesus makes Himself very near. It is also in these moments that the hardness of our heart is chipped away as humility grips our soul and softens our heart so they can be open and usable to our Maker. Sometimes honesty invites tears, but it always pushes us and others back to Jesus. It is the relationships that have walked through the tough conversations that outlast the circumstances life brings. Being honest may invite temporary pain, rejection, hardship, or punishment, but the consequences of willingly compromising our integrity are far greater. Honesty is the process of continually putting our trust in God and knowing that His grace is enough.

So, let's be honest—with ourselves, others, God, and the world around us. Honesty will give space for lasting, true relationships and put us back in our rightful place at the feet of Jesus, where we belong.

FOCUS TIP: Is there a hard conversation you need to have? This is the week to do just that. God loves you, and He loves the truth. Be bold, ask God to be with you, and be honest.

If we claim to have fellowship with him and yet walk in the darkness, we lie and do not live out the truth.
1 JOHN 1:6 NIV

The Lᴏʀᴅ detests lying lips, but He delights in people who are trustworthy.
PROVERBS 12:22 NIV

For we aim at what is honorable not only in the Lord's sight but also in the sight of man.
II CORINTHIANS 8:21 ESV

Whoever walks in integrity walks securely, but whoever takes crooked paths will be found out.
PROVERBS 10:9 NIV

▼

Jesus, I choose honesty, even when it's hard. Amen.

Silence

*Call to Me and I will answer you and tell you great
and unsearchable things you do not know.*
JEREMIAH 33:3 NIV

Microsoft created an anechoic chamber in Redmond, Washington, where their hardware laboratories are based. It is currently the quietest place in the world. Made of concrete walls, they say that if a jet were taking off outside the building, one might hear a faint whisper of noise. It would seem that in a world claiming to yearn for silence amid the noise, people would flock to go inside. However, most visitors have experienced anything but delight. Because we are so used to having background noise, psychologists have compared experiencing this chamber to walking into a dark room. The silence is uncomfortable and alarming, as you can hear your own heartbeat and the breath forming inside your lungs.

How often do we give ourselves opportunities to experience silence? Maybe not to the extreme of the Microsoft chamber, but moments where we don't turn on the television, a podcast, or music. The phone is put away, the computer is set aside, and we just allow silence to exist. The thought of this makes most of us uncomfortable. The moment all things turn off around us is the moment we search for something else to turn on. We claim to hate the noise and desire a break, but this break usually requires us to find rest within ourselves. Sure, the physical exhaustion is never good for us, but what if the real issue is the restlessness inside our souls and the inability to sit still long enough to listen? What if all the noise around us is keeping us from hearing the very clarity we are searching after?

Listening will never come naturally to a culture obsessed with hearing their own voices. When we have the revelation that He is the only One worth listening to, we will make time to hear Him. We will put down technology and take a walk. We will put away the list and honor the Sabbath. We will get enough sleep so that when we rise, we can read the instruction He has already given us in His Word. We will schedule margin so that our soul is given the bandwidth to receive and apply.

Sitting in silence will be uncomfortable sometimes, but wisdom says we should get comfortable with being uncomfortable. Nothing is richer than a life of peace. May we take time to sit in silence so we can hear the One who is capable of giving it.

FOCUS TIP: This week, take time at least once a day to sit in silence, turn off the technology, and listen.

*Whatever you have learned or received or heard
from me, or seen in me—put it into practice.
And the God of peace will be with you.*
PHILIPPIANS 4:9 NIV

*Listen for GOD's voice in everything you do, everywhere
you go; He's the One who will keep you on track.*
PROVERBS 3:6 THE MESSAGE

*Consequently, faith comes from hearing the message, and
the message is heard through the Word about Christ.*
ROMANS 10:17 NIV

*My sheep hear my voice, and I know them, and they
follow me. I give them eternal life, and they will never
perish, and no one will snatch them out of my hand.*
JOHN 10:27–28 ESV

*Jesus, turning down all else,
I'm listening to You. Amen.*

Pace

Whoever keeps his word, in him truly the love of God is perfected.
By this we may know that we are in him: whoever says he abides
in him ought to walk in the same way in which he walked.

I JOHN 2:5–6 ESV

When people train for a marathon, they run at a pace they are able to sustain throughout the entire race. While they could easily sprint at the beginning, they realize that there are hills and hurdles up ahead. Marathons require both perseverance and wisdom, knowing when to exert more energy and when to reserve one's strength.

Many times we treat our faith more like a sprint and less like a marathon. We dash ahead, hoping to race to the finish line before those around us and prove our worth to bystanders. We expel our energy within the first few miles and wonder why all our stamina is gone when we need it most. We allowed the rush around us to cause a rush inside us and our pace to get off, making us compromise the reward of peace for the sake of our pride. In turn, we end up losing both.

Scripture tells us to "run the race" He has set before us, giving all that we can to each moment but trusting Him with our lack. His Word reminds us to stay in our lane, not looking to the right or to the left, which causes us to get our focus off the One we are running toward.

This marathon picture reminds us of Jesus, who we see was never in a hurry. He felt the urgency to share the

Good News, but urgency and hurry are very different. Urgency awakens the soul, requiring the person to be accountable to live in a way that reflects the truth they well know. Hurry confuses the soul, alerting it to the fact that time is of the essence but providing no clarity about which direction to run.

As Jesus walked this earth, He allowed His pace to ebb and flow. He was open to the interruptions of those who needed Him, and His pace allowed Him to serve in the present while never losing sight of what His Father had in store for Him. What if we allowed ourselves to take this same approach? Surely if Jesus did not rush around, we do not have more important things to do, right? Let's slow our pace so that we can walk in peace and prioritize what actually matters.

FOCUS TIP: When you find yourself running full speed ahead this week, remember the word *pace* and ask God to help you to walk in peace.

*For to this you have been called, because Christ
also suffered for you, leaving you an example,
so that you might follow in his steps.*
I PETER 2:21 ESV

*Let your eyes look directly forward, and
your gaze be straight before you.*
PROVERBS 4:25 ESV

*Therefore, since we are surrounded by such a huge
crowd of witnesses to the life of faith, let us strip
off every weight that slows us down, especially the
sin that so easily trips us up. And let us run with
endurance the race God has set before us.*
HEBREWS 12:1 NLT

*Now may the Lord of peace Himself give you peace at
all times and in every way. The Lord be with all of you.*
II THESSALONIANS 3:16 NIV

▼

*Jesus, determine my pace
and guide my feet. Amen.*

▸ taking inventory:

LITTLE

1. How did your *little* make a difference in the kingdom?

2. Have you ever felt paralyzed by possibility? How did you move past this feeling?

3. Think of a little thing someone did that had a big impact on your life. How did God work to make that little thing strengthen you?

HONESTY

1. God tells us in Proverbs that "the Lord detests lying lips" (12:22 NIV). When you focused on *honesty*, did a certain situation come to mind?

2. Think about your relationships. Has honesty proven to be a crucial component of a strong foundation?

3. Did you find the courage to be honest even when it wasn't comfortable? Did God help you through it?

SILENCE

1. Have you ever tried to talk to someone who is more interested in something other than your conversation? What if the Holy Spirit is trying to communicate with you but your attention is elsewhere?

2. Instead of listening to the only One capable of giving peace, what do you listen to? Whose voice do you turn up the loudest in your life?

3. Is there a place or practice you can do that helps you become silent so you can listen more easily? If so, what is it?

PACE

1. Is your pride related to your pace?

2. Did you catch yourself when "hurry" overtook you? How did you let go of hurrying?

3. Did you notice that your pace was directly related to your peace?

Dear Jesus, thank You for meeting me exactly where I am and giving me all that I need to serve You well. Help me know that my little steps of obedience are all that You ask of me. Show me how to lay it all at Your feet and trust You with the outcome. Step by step, I follow You. Thank You for the freedom to be honest with myself, others, and You. I never need to hide the truth; You will love me through it all. Lord, I love that You care enough to help me step away from the noise. I want to listen to You. Help me remove the distractions and turn down all else. You are faithful to speak. Your example to insistently obey while never compromising Your peace is set all throughout Your Word. It proves that I can be mission-minded while still being present-focused. Keep me in line with You. In Jesus' name, amen.

Release

Brothers and sisters, I do not consider myself yet to have taken hold of it. But one thing I do: Forgetting what is behind and straining toward what is ahead.

PHILIPPIANS 3:13 NIV

Isn't it strange how we feel the need to give credence to beliefs, patterns, or habits we used to have? Like a really hard breakup—you know it's best for you and what you've been holding onto is only hurting you, but the actual stepping away and turning from what you've attached yourself to for so long, well, it's downright difficult.

And you think: *How can I redeem it?* Like trying to gain control of the past, which we all know is impossible and slightly looney tunes (but we do it regardless). Or we experience nostalgia about those old lanes we used to drive down. We are really good at romanticizing what we used to attach ourselves to because it makes it easier to explain to ourselves why we held on for so long. And in allowing ourselves to mentally backtrack, we often allow that worthlessness or shame or guilt to begin its usual soundtrack.

But here's the thing: we owe nothing to what we used to believe about anything. We don't have to explain to ourselves or to anyone around us the whys or the whats or the hows. But what we must do is remind our heart that anything our mind remembers, God has already redeemed. Any thought pattern, lie, or struggle we have had, we get to move forward in a different way. And how is that? By stepping into the truth.

If we want our mind to cling to new beliefs, we must truly let go of old ones.

If we want our heart to be open to love in our present, we must release broken promises from our past.

If we want our soul to experience the goodness God has for our future, we are going to have to trust that He really does redeem and restore everything.

The release is always a little scary. We naturally prefer the security of holding something, and sometimes the wait of what will be or how it will feel is hard. The uncertainty of a new chapter is often what makes closing an old chapter so difficult. However, until we release what has been holding us, we will not be able to experience the anticipation of the bright, exciting future God has in store. We know our best is ahead of us, so may we run forth, releasing all that is behind.

FOCUS TIP: This week, when feelings of shame or uncertainty start to come to mind, think of the word *release* and ask God to fill you with His love, comfort, and peace instead.

Therefore, if anyone is in Christ, he is a new creation. The old has passed away; behold, the new has come.

II CORINTHIANS 5:17 ESV

Whoever conceals their sins does not prosper, but the one who confesses and renounces them finds mercy.

PROVERBS 28:13 NIV

Even to your old age, I am He, and even to gray hairs I will carry you! I have made, and I will bear; even I will carry, and will deliver you.

ISAIAH 46:4 NKJV

Turn your burdens over to the LORD, and He will take care of you. He will never let the righteous person stumble.

PSALM 55:22 GW

▼

Jesus, what I release, You redeem. Amen.

Prayer

*This is the confidence we have in approaching God: that
if we ask anything according to His will, He hears us.*
I JOHN 5:14 NIV

If you knew you had the magic password to enter a new level of success, would you use it? If you knew you had the key to access a fulfilling life, would you tap into it? If you knew you had a way to teleport into heavenly places, would you regularly go there? These seem like rhetorical questions, all offering a new way of experiencing life and blessings. Of course we would utilize these things if we had them, right?

Well, we do, but the magic password, key, and teleporting device all form a three-in-one tool, and that tool is called *prayer*. Maybe because we have linked prayer to church, sickness, or premeal time, we associate it with formality or tradition, but prayer is the most powerful tool we have on this side of heaven. It is our direct line to the Father, and when we pray to Him, He listens. We don't have to put in a request or stand in line; He truly bends down to listen to the prayers of His children, big or small.

What would our lives look like if prayer became our way of life rather than our life support? Prayer is the portal to success of every kind; it is also in the communication of prayer and understanding our Father's heart that we learn what true success means. Prayer allows us to experience God in deeper and more intimate ways. When we ask for spiritual gifts so that we can take part in kingdom work, God meets us there. Our prayers are powerful, authoritative, and significant.

Sure, prayer can be the way that our soul sings itself to sleep, but it was never meant to dull our senses; it is actually the quickest way to become fully alive in Jesus. If we allowed prayer to become our go-to response in both frustration and celebration, in tragedy and triumph, in seeking wisdom in the big and the small—we would see that God is always available to hear the voices of His children. And the more we turn to Him, the more our heart look like His.

FOCUS TIP: This week, surround yourself with the word *prayer*. Put it on a sticky note at work, write it on your bathroom mirror, set a reminder on your phone, jot it down in your weekly planner—and pray your heart out every time you see the word. Pray about every detail of your life. Nothing is too small to discuss with God. He cares about every detail.

*Do not be anxious about anything, but in everything
by prayer and supplication with thanksgiving
let your requests be made known to God.*

PHILIPPIANS 4:6 ESV

*Pray in the Spirit on all occasions with all kinds of
prayers and requests. With this in mind, be alert and
always keep on praying for all the Lord's people.*

EPHESIANS 6:18 NIV

*Is anyone among you in trouble? Let them pray. Is
anyone happy? Let them sing songs of praise.*

JAMES 5:13 NIV

*Therefore I tell you, whatever you ask for in prayer,
believe that you have received it, and it will be yours.*

MARK 11:24 NIV

*Jesus, help me pray.
I know You're listening. Amen.*

Joy

You make known to me the path of life; in your presence there is fullness of joy; at your right hand are pleasures forevermore.
PSALM 16:11 ESV

I s there someone in your life who just oozes joy? Sun-shine or rain, they offer a positivity that you crave being around. Even when hard things happen or the unexpected occurs, they have a way of being sad that is still hopeful and rooted in joy, knowing their story is being written by Someone much greater. It is as though they have decided that their joy will simply not be snatched.

Wouldn't it be awesome if this was how the world viewed Christ-followers? If we lived with gratitude, operated in the hope that doesn't fade, and pursued righteousness, joy would be our continual posture. And shouldn't it be? We claim to follow the One who has saved us from ourselves, given us purpose for our present, and established a secure future in eternity—and yet we often seem empty. The words we say begin to fall flat when it appears as if a vacuum has come in and sucked out all the joy from our lives. The truth is, if we believe that the message of the gospel is true, our entire lives should be expressions of joy, because everything we receive, including our very breath, is living grace.

Which would be more effective, a person who speaks highly of Jesus and His joy or someone who lives every day with joy, letting their beliefs be the source of their hope?

It is one thing to talk about joy amid heartache; it is completely another to choose joy when tragedy knocks at your own front door. Our lives are our greatest sermon, and the watching world is looking for something to hold onto! They want to see what we do when we fall, who we turn to when we are rejected, how we handle success, what we build our lives upon, and whether we still walk in the same joy on the hard days as we do on the good days. It is our everyday, seemingly unimportant moments that have the opportunity to communicate a life-changing message to those around us.

Our joy must be unexpected and contagious—unexpected when we operate in joy and life feels hard, and contagious when the celebration of our joy cannot be contained. May others who see our lives never have to ask whether we believe in Jesus because our joy so obviously will be because of Him. Much like all the gifts our Father offers us, the more we choose the joy of eternity, the more joy will make itself known while we're here.

FOCUS TIP: As you focus on the word *joy* this week, remember that no matter what happens, we have Jesus, and that alone fills our hearts with never-ending delight.

You haven't done this before. Ask, using My name, and
you will receive, and you will have abundant joy.
JOHN 16:24 NLT

Your statutes are my heritage forever;
they are the joy of my heart.
PSALM 119:111 NIV

Though you have not seen him, you love him. Though you
do not now see him, you believe in him and rejoice with
joy that is inexpressible and filled with glory, obtaining
the outcome of your faith, the salvation of your souls.
I PETER 1:8–9 ESV

Rejoice in the Lord always; again I will say, rejoice.
PHILIPPIANS 4:4 ESV

▼

Jesus, because I have You,
I always have joy. Amen.

Movement

Therefore I urge you, brethren, by the mercies of God, to
present your bodies a living and holy sacrifice, acceptable
to God, which is your spiritual service of worship.
ROMANS 12:1 NASB

Frustrated. Snappy. My husband had not done anything wrong, but I found myself deeply annoyed with the situation at hand. *Why can't I snap out of it?* I thought to myself, knowing my answer before I did much evaluating. Due to my overcommitment at work, I was not leaving myself as much time to work out like I usually do. I was frustrated physically, yes, but I noticed the difference more in my mindset. My perspective was not as centered, I was more easily distracted, and I knew I wasn't giving my body the attention it deserved so that my mind, heart, and spirit could get aligned.

Research proves that I am not alone in this. A recent Harvard study confirmed that those who participated in some type of activity five times a week were far less likely to experience a range of medical issues, naturally felt happier, and were better able to respond to life's curveballs because of the resilience they had built up through physical activity.

When we think of movement, we tend to think only in terms of extremes, therefore making any change feel defeating or impossible. But movement is less about how far we are walking and more about walking in gratitude that our bodies can move and take us places. Will we always feel like moving? Absolutely not, but we do not always have to feel like doing something in order to know that it is good for us. When, we begin moving, as our heart rate increases and our blood starts to flow, our mind responds and gets on board. When our body, brain, and our spirit works together and helps encourage one another to stay healthy and in motion, we become powerful forces for the kingdom.

When we want to crawl into a hole and avoid the hurdle in front of us, we can choose to walk outside, feel the sunshine on our face, and allow what we visibly see to establish greater trust in what we cannot see. Movement gets our blood flowing so that our mind can better handle the reality of our situation while letting the reality of heaven be our guide. It requires us to persevere when we come up against moments that we deem too difficult or we want to physically stop. Sometimes it is in the physical that we realize the potential of Jesus within us, and this revelation helps us sort through our emotions and persevere mentally.

Move. Get outside of yourself and do diligence to the gift of life you've been given. Moving *your* feet helps you put everything else at *His* feet.

FOCUS TIP: This week when you find yourself frustrated or snappy, think *movement* and then walk away. Go for a quick run on the treadmill, attend that workout class you've been missing, or simply take a walk around the park.

Do you not know that your bodies are temples of the
Holy Spirit, who is in you, whom you have received
from God? You are not your own; you were bought
at a price. Therefore honor God with your bodies.

I CORINTHIANS 6:19–20 NIV

Now may the God of peace Himself sanctify
you entirely; and may your spirit and soul and
body be preserved complete, without blame
at the coming of our Lord Jesus Christ.

I THESSALONIANS 5:23 NASB

If Christ is in you, though the body is dead because of sin,
yet the spirit is alive because of righteousness. But if the
Spirit of Him who raised Jesus from the dead dwells in you,
He who raised Christ Jesus from the dead will also give life
to your mortal bodies through His Spirit who dwells in you.

ROMANS 8:10–11 NASB

So whether you eat or drink or whatever
you do, do it all for the glory of God.

I CORINTHIANS 10:31 NIV

▼

Jesus, when I move,
I feel You work. Amen.

▶ taking inventory:

RELEASE

1. What burdens did you release to the Lord?

2. You cannot change the past or control the future. How, then, should you spend the present?

3. Were you able to release something from your past? Have you seen the benefits of letting it go?

PRAYER

1. Do you truly believe that God hears your prayers?

2. How often do you pray because you are happy? Why would God like to hear from you in those times?

3. Did you pray for wisdom or discernment? What was the outcome?

JOY

1. Did you think of a friend, teacher, or colleague who walks in joy consistently? Were you able to learn from them?

2. Did you notice anything that tended to override your joy? Were you able to overcome that and concentrate on bringing more joy to your life?

3. What did God reveal about Himself as you focused on being joyful?

MOVEMENT

1. Did you notice that adding physical activity to your life helped strengthen your faith?

2. Did you notice changes throughout the week? Did adding movement to your schedule invigorate your soul?

3. How will you be integrating movement into your schedule in the weeks and years to come?

*Dear Jesus, thank You for championing
my future and giving grace to my present
by redeeming my past; there is nothing
too big or too heavy that I am not able to
release in Your name. Give me the courage
to move forward and choose new paths.
Jesus, through prayer, You not only give me
power and authority but also allow me to
deeply feel and experience Your love and
care. Help me, Father, to turn to You and
surrender everything to You. I am listening.
Thank You for the joy that follows
when I follow You. Even on the hard
days, the hope of heaven anchors
me in joy that is unexplainable.
Thank You for delighting in me.
I am filled with gratitude for the gift
of my physical body and all the things
that I am capable of doing in You.
Help me to be consistent and show up
in this area; re-center my mind and
guard my heart as I move my feet.
In Jesus' name, amen.*

Rooted

Then Christ will make His home in your hearts as you trust in Him.
Your roots will grow down into God's love and keep you strong.

EPHESIANS 3:17 NLT

What is the difference between a tree and a bush? Seems like a rhetorical question when we are thinking about what our eyes physically see. A tree stands tall above the ground, and a bush is more stubby in appearance, lacking the ability to sprout large limbs or grow much in stature. This tangible difference is obvious, but it is the invisible difference between these two that is the true mark: their root system. Trees have deep root systems, anchoring them into the earth beneath them and securing their stability amid the winds and storms that are sure to come their way. This root system allows trees to withstand the four changing seasons. Even though they may differ in appearance from summer to winter, they are still processing and living. It is their foundation that allows them to be planted in difficult spaces.

It is the same with our faith—we can be beautiful to the eye, visibly impressive to a passerby; however, it is what is underneath the surface that impresses our Father. If we want to be rooted in our faith, then we must know the One we claim to follow. In order to know someone, we must spend time with them. In other words, the only way to deepen and widen our root system is to bury ourselves in the soil of His Word. We must educate the heart on who He is and His character. We must read the stories of those who have gone before us, who survived winter and the harshest of storms. What did they cling to? What did Jesus tell them?

If by grace we grow tall and strong in stature but sow our roots into human wisdom or personal power, we will begin to wilt at the first sight of a true storm. When the unexpected occurs, it is what we are tied to—our roots—that we will ultimately depend on. That is also what roots do: they draw nutrients from the soil. When we have a healthy root system, we tap into nourishment in many different ways. Through the central life-giving source of Jesus, we are obedient in connecting ourselves to His power system—the body of Christ. We involve ourselves in community, we intentionally serve, we plant ourselves in a church, and we find ways to encourage and be refreshed in Jesus. This provides us with soul nutrients, knowing that we are rooted in deep relationship, which is the heart of His kingdom.

We do not become tall, flourishing trees to impress others with ourselves; we become tall, flourishing trees to remind others of what it looks like to be rooted in Jesus. It is the foundation, what is underneath, that is the life-giving source of all the things we do see.

FOCUS TIP: This week, before responding in anger or sarcasm or spite, think or whisper the word *rooted* and stand firm, remembering that your response to that person or situation has more to do with you being rooted in Christ than it does with the situation at hand.

*Blessed is the one who trusts in the L*ORD*, whose confidence is in Him. They will be like a tree planted by the water that sends out its roots by the stream. It does not fear when heat comes; its leaves are always green. It has no worries in a year of drought and never fails to bear fruit.*

JEREMIAH 17:7–8 NIV

I am the vine; you are the branches. If you remain in Me and I in you, you will bear much fruit; apart from Me you can do nothing.

JOHN 15:5 NIV

So then, just as you received Christ Jesus as Lord, continue to live your lives in Him, rooted and built up in him, strengthened in the faith as you were taught, and overflowing with thankfulness.

COLOSSIANS 2:6–7 NIV

But when the sun came up, the plants were scorched, and they withered because they had no root.

MATTHEW 13:6 NIV

▼

*Jesus, rooted in You,
I stand secure. Amen.*

Restoration

*Jerusalem will be rebuilt on its ruins, and
the palace reconstructed as before.*

JEREMIAH 30:18 NLT

Did we read that verse correctly? "Jerusalem will be rebuilt on its ruins . . ."? This Scripture refers to when Jerusalem had been destroyed by the Romans and was in desolate condition. The chaos and struggle that had taken place in this land was undeniable, and yet God says this was exactly where He wanted to rebuild—upon the rubble.

Isn't that exactly what God does with us? We have these places of brokenness in our lives, and we desperately want to run from them, cover them, and pretend they never existed. The memories of "what was" still ring in our minds and it feels too hard to stay in this place, and yet God calls us back here. As we look at ground zero, we wonder how He could possibly build upon this many broken pieces; yet that is His specialty. It is usually in the exact spaces we label "ruined" where He rewrites and stamps "restored." The fullness of His redemption is most evident when the shattering is most apparent.

- The relationship or friendship we have written off.
- The marriage we desperately want to walk away from.
- The health issues that are stealing our energy.
- The addiction that has claimed so much of our time.

- The childhood we refuse to let go of but hate to remember.
- The battle we fight to be joyful on a daily basis.

The failure. The hurt. The pain. However it looks, however long it has been there, however it came to be, that place—that is Jerusalem. The site that we label as unfixable is the same location He yearns to restore. Our brokenness was never supposed to numb our feet, making us so used to walking on rubble that we hardly flinch when we are cut. It was supposed to wake us up to imperfection, to make us yearn for something more, and realize that only He can place our feet on safe land.

May we be okay with inviting others and our own heart into the depths of our depravity, realizing that giving light to our struggles becomes the pen to write our redemption story. And in the space where we find refuge, we become a resource for others. It is often in the places of our greatest pain—our ruins—that God wants to conduct His greatest reconstruction.

FOCUS TIP: Do you feel broken today? Do you feel confident that God will restore your current circumstance and make something beautiful out of your ashes? This week, every time you start to think that nothing good will come from it, say the word *restoration* and know that He never breaks His promises. We just have to hold on and watch.

He heals the brokenhearted and binds up their wounds.

PSALM 147:3 NIV

Thus says the One who is high and lifted up, who inhabits eternity, whose name is Holy: "I dwell in the high and holy place, and also with him who is of a contrite and lowly spirit, to revive the spirit of the lowly, and to revive the heart of the contrite."

ISAIAH 57:15 ESV

O LORD, if you heal me, I will be truly healed; if You save me, I will be truly saved. My praises are for You alone?

JEREMIAH 17:14 NLT

In His kindness God called you to share in His eternal glory by means of Christ Jesus. So after you have suffered a little while, He will restore, support, and strengthen you, and He will place you on a firm foundation.

I PETER 5:10 NLT

▼

*Jesus, in my brokenness,
You restore. Amen.*

Stay

Be watchful, stand firm in the faith, act like men, be strong.

I CORINTHIANS 16:13 ESV

We always talk about *going* because going is often more alluring, more exciting, than staying. We want to try new things! We want to be adventurous. *Going* feels as if we are activating our gifts, utilizing our resources, and walking into new spaces. But *staying?* Staying is hard. It is often the last thing we want to do, because when we are praying about transition or uncertainty, it is usually prompted by a restlessness or frustration with our present, right? We want to walk away and start fresh or exit the current situation/relationship and participate in something that feels more worthy of our time.

However, it is often *staying* that grows us the most. Staying requires us to die to ourselves and our own perception of what is important, fun, or relevant. It strips us of the ability to leave or avoid and forces us to remain and confront. Throughout Scripture, Jesus asks His people to stay and fight in times when it did not make sense. Chaos might be ensuing, the harvest might not seem to be coming, and it might seem reasonable to go. But Jesus knew that if they kept their feet in that same space, dependence would be their only remedy.

What if Jesus is asking us to stay in certain spaces in our lives so that we can rely solely on His strength to keep us there? Whether it be physically staying in a city that we want to leave due to an unforeseen circumstance or remaining in a conversation we want to avoid because it makes us uncomfortable, where is it in our lives that Jesus might be asking us to stay?

Above all, there is certainly one place He continually wants us to stay: in Him. Abiding, seeking refuge, pursuing wholeness, constantly seeking His guidance, and receiving His love. It is only in our discipline to stay in the shadow of His wings that we gain the courage to soar anywhere else.

When our heart experiences the peace and our eyes see the power of keeping ourselves locked in place, even when it feels like work and tastes like obedience, we will understand that in order to go far, we must stay in His will.

FOCUS TIP: This week, ask God where and in what ways He wants you to stay still. And every time you feel compelled to start taking those situations into your own hands, close your eyes and whisper the word *stay*. Be ready to feel a sense of peace as your grip loosens and your heart stops beating a mile a minute, and you'll know that being still was the right move.

No temptation has overtaken you that is not common to man. God is faithful, and he will not let you be tempted beyond your ability, but with the temptation he will also provide the way of escape, that you may be able to endure it.

I CORINTHIANS 10:13 ESV

God is not unjust so as to overlook your work and the love that you have shown for his name in serving the saints, as you still do.

HEBREWS 6:10 ESV

I do not account my life of any value nor as precious to myself, if only I may finish my course and the ministry that I received from the Lord Jesus, to testify to the gospel of the grace of God.

ACTS 20:24 ESV

You have need of endurance, so that when you have done the will of God you may receive what is promised.

HEBREWS 10:36 ESV

▼

Jesus, I will stay where You instruct.
Peace will be mine. Amen.

Refreshed

He restores my soul. He leads me in paths of
righteousness for his name's sake.

PSALM 23:3 ESV

Remember those hot summer days when we ran through the sprinklers or grabbed the water hose in an effort to counteract our sweat from playing outside for hours? But the water hitting our bodies wasn't enough to quench our thirst, right? We then ran inside for some water or hoped Mom was on her way with a Gatorade to help us out.

And yet, when it comes to the Word of God, we try to run past the water hose and pray *that* quenches our thirst. We hope that the few drops we catch in our mouths will sustain as we continue our usual regimen, but we end up exhausted. We feel like we are at the end of our rope, but we fear taking time out of our day when we have so much to do. The truth is this—there is no other way to receive true refreshment than to spend time with Jesus. Other solutions will temporarily get us by, but we will soon realize that what we are doing isn't working. Does stopping, sitting down, and drinking some water for ourselves interrupt our schedule? Sure. But it is also the only way we will know what is worth filling our schedule. In other words, if we do not take the time to fill ourselves with the discernment, wisdom, and power of the Holy Spirit inside of us, we will have no idea how to direct our energy, resources, and time to the outside world. It is our refreshment in Jesus and His Word that provides us with the ability to refresh others.

When we know Jesus, we are allowed to be tired, but we are not being honest with ourselves if we pretend that we don't know where to go to be refreshed. Attending church weekly, going to small group, and listening to podcasts are all great things! But they were never intended to replace the real thing—time with Jesus. He offers refreshment that is far past our physical state; it seeps into the chambers of our heart and pulls us out of those old routines. It transforms our perspective, gives us wisdom in relationships, and simply reminds our heart that we are loved. When we refresh ourselves in Jesus, we stop placing the expectations on our other relationships to quench our thirst as only He can. We also become incredibly refreshing to be around when we have been renewed in Him.

We need this living water every day in order to activate the God-given gifts and dreams inside of us. The spray from the water hose no longer works; let's sit with Him and be refreshed to run our race well.

FOCUS TIP: Wake up every morning this week and ask God to refresh your soul before you start your day.

I will satisfy the weary soul, and every languishing soul I will replenish.
JEREMIAH 31:25 ESV

The law of the Lord is perfect, reviving the soul; the testimony of the Lord is sure, making wise the simple.
PSALM 19:7 ESV

Be not wise in your own eyes; fear the Lord, and turn away from evil. It will be healing to your flesh and refreshment to your bones.
PROVERBS 3:7–8 ESV

Repent, then, and turn to God, so that your sins may be wiped out, that times of refreshing may come from the Lord.
ACTS 3:19 NIV

▼

*Jesus, when I drink,
You refresh me. Amen.*

▶ taking inventory:

ROOTED

1. The blessed one will be like a tree "planted by the water" (Jeremiah 17:7-8 NIV). Have you watered your root system?

2. Where do you tend to look for security and strength? How can you strengthen your roots?

3. Is there someone in your life who has a really strong foundation? Can you lean on them to learn how to stay grounded?

RESTORATION

1. What heartaches and wounds did you ask God to heal?

2. Focus on these verbs from Scripture: heal, bind up, revive, restore, support, strengthen, place on a firm foundation. Did you see any of these taking place the week you focused on restoration?

3. Have you noticed others using their brokenness to deepen their empathy and make them stronger? Have you encouraged them?

STAY

1. Where do you have need of endurance? Where does God want you to stay?

2. As you focused on staying in His will, how did each day feel lighter?

3. Do you trust that God can get you to where He wants you to go?

REFRESHED

1. Does your mind, heart, soul, or body need refreshment?

2. What's the most realistic change you've made in order to spend more time with Jesus?

3. Did being refreshed take time?

*Dear Jesus, thank You for providing me
with Your presence and Your Word—it is the
surest foundation. Help me to anchor myself
in You and Your promises, not letting the
storms of life make me doubt Your faithfulness.
I love the way You invite, accept, and restore
my brokenness. Help me to never be afraid to
let the light in, knowing that You are never
afraid of rubble. Great is Your faithfulness.
Thank You for Your direction and guidance.
When You call me to stay, give me the courage
and boldness to remain. Help me to stay and
get comfortable with being uncomfortable.
I'm locked in place, with my eyes on You.
You refresh my mind, heart, soul, and body.
There is no substitute for You or Your Word.
Help me to remember to drink from it on
a daily basis—it is the source of life.
In Jesus' name, amen.*

Cultivate

May the favor of the Lord our God rest on us; establish the work of our hands for us—yes, establish the work of our hands.

PSALM 90:17 NIV

We are inherently cultivators—we put our hands to different things, giving our mental energy to those efforts, and we spend time hoping that things will come forth to fruition in due time. We never have to wonder whether we are capable of cultivating; we are made to do so. Rather, the question is, what are we cultivating, and is that what we want our legacy to be about?

It is strange how we often spend our time doing one thing but hope our life is full of something else. We want the blessing without giving the intentionality and discipline required to have that blessing. We water seeds of discouragement and wonder why we aren't chasing our dreams. We try to fit every kind of flower and vegetable into our garden, desiring "all the things," and then wonder why our soil can't support the growth. This attempt to have everything makes it impossible for anything to thrive because every plant begins to steal nutrients from another in order to survive. Frustrated and defeated, we learn the hard way that we were never meant to do everything. We were designed to pursue certain things and do them well, giving adequate care and time to each one.

What is growing in the garden of your life right now?

Whatever it is does not have to remain, but removing roots is hard work. Replacing the weeds will require some digging, dirty hands, and diligent care, but it is the only way we can make room for things that give us life.

Cultivating joy is usually preceded by obedience. Cultivating peace is often attained by planting seeds of solitude. Cultivating courage to pursue our dreams usually looks like plowing the field and still showing up when the harvest feels distant. And the beautiful flowers, fruits, and plants that are thriving? Celebrate how they have cultivated and rejoice in the benefit of hard work and faith.

Perfect planting weather will not always be in the cards. Beginning a new season will always feel difficult. Implementing a new rhythm that slows the soul and allows time for growth will sometimes feel counterproductive. But we can trust that when we unearth our purpose in Jesus and begin to plant what matters to Him, He will give us all we need to flourish. As we cultivate with Jesus, our focus will turn from the harvest to the process and our heart will be reminded that our true reward is in daily trusting Him.

FOCUS TIP: This week, think through what you might want to cultivate in your life. Do you need more courage or strength? Do you need to feel joy again, or to feel loved and comforted? Ask God to give you everything you need today and to show you the ways to grow closer and closer Him.

*A time to give birth and a time to die; a time to
plant and a time to uproot what is planted.*
ECCLESIASTES 3:2 NASB

*He who tills his land will have plenty of food, but he who
follows empty pursuits will have poverty in plenty.*
PROVERBS 28:19 NASB

*Let us not become weary in doing good, for at the proper
time we will reap a harvest if we do not give up.*
GALATIANS 6:9 NIV

No word from God will ever fail.
LUKE 1:37 BSB

*Jesus, help me to discern.
I want to cultivate
what matters. Amen.*

Illuminate

In the same way, let your light shine before others,
so that they may see your good works and give
glory to your Father who is in heaven.

MATTHEW 5:16 ESV

Merriam-Webster Dictionary defines *illuminate* as "to supply or brighten with light, to make clear." When we think of the term "illuminate," a light bulb usually comes to mind, or providing light to a space. As I thought about this word, the portion of the definition that says "to make clear" really made me think. Our job as His children is to make the love of our Father clear. When we enter a room, is our presence giving clarity to what it means to be loved by Jesus? Do our words, actions, and lives help open the eyes of others to His supernatural kindness and grace?

I think this word gets the short end of the stick, as people begin to define illuminating as "shining" and shining can sometimes seem shallow, as though it's based on human accolades or achievement. However, when we define it in relation to how Jesus illuminates, there is an immediate depth that is present. The light that comes forth is not just one of joy or delight, but one that provides guidance and discernment. The Word of Jesus is what illuminates our path and gives us wisdom to know when to go right and when to turn left. This clarity, as we seek to have the eyes of Jesus, is always founded upon truth. Illumination is what paves the way for revelation and transformation. It is through the process of illumination that our eyes are opened to the way we should rightly see others, providing a richness in relationships that only He can provide.

How would our lives change if we thought less about influencing others and more about illuminating Jesus? There would be less pressure on our shoulders and more expectations on Him to show up. We would not be depending on our own capability to lead, because we know the only way to bring light to a situation is to invite Jesus in. His exposure, intimacy, and peace are what transform an atmosphere. Our concern would be less about our reputation and more about the future of those we love. The most attractive quality about a person will always be their devotion to their Maker. It is this commitment a person makes that allows them to have a greater impact on others and be an example of what it looks like to open one's heart to Jesus.

As we envelop ourselves in relationship with Him, illumination is the result. We pursue the light, and in turn we become a light in the darkness and bring glory to His name.

FOCUS TIP: Look for ways to illuminate Jesus in all you do this week.

Now I have heard about you that a spirit of the gods is in you, and that illumination, insight and extraordinary wisdom have been found in you.

DANIEL 5:14 NASB

There was the true Light which, coming into the world, enlightens every man.

JOHN 1:9 NASB

I pray that the eyes of your heart may be enlightened, so that you will know what is the hope of His calling, what are the riches of the glory of His inheritance in the saints.

EPHESIANS 1:18 NASB

Your eye is like a lamp that provides light for your body. When your eye is healthy, your whole body is filled with light. But when it is unhealthy, your body is filled with darkness.

LUKE 11:34 NLT

▼

Jesus, when I abide,
You illuminate. Amen.

Courage

Be strong, and let your heart take courage,
all you who wait for the LORD!
PSALM 31:24 ESV

It's this weird thing—we sometimes think that if we use up all the courage we have inside, we won't have any for what's next, for what's ahead. And we know we will need some then.

And so we hesitantly walk forward, making sure to keep some in our reserve tank for tomorrow, right? Much like creativity, we are convinced that we are running on limited supply. And so we have taught ourselves to use it sparingly. We fear that if we bravely execute in this moment, we will be expected to be brave in the next and what if we can't do what's next?

But you know what I have found to be true? The more courage we use, the more we will find. The more we walk forward in faith, the quicker we will be able to take the step next time. The more we choose to trust God with our next step, the more we will be able to trust Him with the next, next step.

And then the one after. That's what is so beautiful and exciting about courage—we will never run out! Because the source of where it's coming from is a well that does not run dry—this faith tank that just replenishes itself over and over.

And the more exciting part? The more we become people of courage, the bolder our steps become and the deeper into the brush we can go. We peel back the leaves of uncertainty and stop searching for safety nets before we propel ourselves into the beauty and grace found in the unknown. Our experience teaches us that we do not need to see human footprints on the paths we walk because the Savior of the world has walked every path before us. *And* better yet: He is walking with us, depositing courage as we go.

But we must walk forward in order to know the courage that lies within us.

We must do that thing, pursue that dream, have that conversation, make that confession, forgive that person—we must decide to do it. If we wait to feel courageous, we will often let the voices of uncertainty and doubt speak so loudly that our feet forget we are equipped to be exactly where we are. The lion will roar too loud and we will shrink back, forgetting that we represent the One who shut the mouth of lions for Daniel and protected David from lions in the pastures. We can operate in courage in our present because our future cannot be harmed by an enemy that has no control over it unless we give it to him.

Confinement and comfort were never meant to be the themes of our lives. But courage? Oh yes. And the more we use, the more we have. Unlimited supply, that is His promise.

Go on. Do not be afraid. Be brave with your life.

FOCUS TIP: When you find yourself afraid this week, remember that God is walking with you, giving you all the courage you need to fulfill your purpose.

*Be strong and of good courage, do not fear nor be
afraid of them; for the L*ORD *your God, He is the One who
goes with you. He will not leave you nor forsake you.*

DEUTERONOMY 31:6 NKJV

*When I am afraid, I will trust in You. In God,
whose word I praise, in God I trust; I will not be
afraid. What can mere mortals do to me?*

PSALM 56:3–4 CSB

*The L*ORD *is my light and my salvation; whom shall I fear? The
L*ORD *is the strength of my life; of whom shall I be afraid?*

PSALM 27:1 NKJV

*Have I not commanded you? Be strong and courageous.
Do not be afraid; do not be discouraged, for the
L*ORD *your God will be with you wherever you go.*

JOSHUA 1:9 NIV

▼

*Jesus, You are near.
Make me courageous. Amen.*

Beauty

All that is in the world— the desires of the flesh
and the desires of the eyes and pride of life— is
not from the Father but is from the world.

I JOHN 2:16 ESV

How do you determine where you want to go on vacation? Maybe it's the mountains because the views showing the world below are mesmerizing. Or maybe it's the beach, as the waves crash upon the shoreline and the vastness reveals His majesty.

How do you decide which clothes to buy, what house to purchase, or what car to drive? Your taste reveals what you find appealing and pleasing to the eye.

How do you pick your spouse? Surely it's not just their physical appearance, but there is something about them that attracts you and pulls you in.

Beauty is a part of our lives in every facet. The danger with this is that we often let the standards of the world around us, the pressures we place on our own shoulders, and the unrealistic expectations we have formed lead the way. With perfection as the goal and the constant change of what is considered popular, we find ourselves striving, exhausted, and unfulfilled. We are confused as to why this idea of "beauty" never fulfills, provides significance, or helps us feel loved.

This is not a new thing, though. It has actually been a struggle since the beginning of time. Adam and Eve, born out of perfection in the image of God, ate from the one tree in all the Garden that God had instructed them not to touch. Scripture tells us that the enemy lured them in with his deceiving questions, hoping they would let the lust of their eyes overcome their confidence in the Lord: "When the woman saw that the fruit of the tree was good for food and pleasing to the eye, and also desirable for gaining wisdom, she took some and ate it" (Genesis 3:6 NIV).

It's easy to look at Eve and point a finger, but how often do we fall for the glitz and glamour around us? We take a bite of the apple that we know won't satisfy because it just looked so good. But as in the garden, God's idea of beauty is only found from within. It is full of life, without shame, and pure.

How do we pursue beauty in the Lord—in our decisions, our appearance, our relationships, and our heart? We follow His commands, and we keep our eyes fixed on Him. We let that build our trust in His will, knowing that He does not withhold good. We inform our heart of His standards in His Word and let those determine our lives and expectations. Beauty from the inside out, that is His heart. The more we live in His presence and understand how He sees beauty, the more we will see it in others and the world around us.

FOCUS TIP: As you go about your week, ask God to open your eyes to what He sees as beautiful. Remember to thank Him for all the beautiful things He reveals to you.

Your beauty should not come from outward adornment,
such as elaborate hairstyles and the wearing of gold
jewelry or fine clothes. Rather, it should be that of
your inner self, the unfading beauty of a gentle and
quiet spirit, which is of great worth in God's sight.

I PETER 3:3–4 NIV

You are altogether beautiful, my love; there is no flaw in you.

SONG OF SOLOMON 4:7 ESV

The LORD said to Samuel, "Do not look on his appearance
or on the height of his stature, because I have rejected
him. For the LORD sees not as man sees: man looks on the
outward appearance, but the LORD looks on the heart."

I SAMUEL 16:7 ESV

One thing have I asked of the LORD, that will I seek
after: that I may dwell in the house of the LORD all
the days of my life, to gaze upon the beauty of
the LORD and to inquire in his temple.

PSALM 27:4 ESV

Jesus, Your beauty surrounds.
Help me to see. Amen.

▶ taking inventory:

CULTIVATE

1. Both Proverbs and Galatians speak of "empty pursuits." While focusing on *cultivate*, did you become aware of any empty pursuits in your life?

2. Did you find things you wanted to cultivate more of in your life?

3. Did you experience the power of cultivating new ground in your life?

ILLUMINATE

1. Did you find that when you started to pursue the light, you became the light?

2. Is there someone in your life who illuminates God's light well? Did you thank them for being a true example?

3. When focusing on *illuminate*, what changes did you observe in your circumstances?

COURAGE

1. "The LORD your God will be with you wherever you go" (Joshua 1:9 NIV). As you focused on that truth, did you find your courage increasing?

2. The focus on illumination links closely with the focus on courage: "The LORD is my light and salvation—whom shall I fear?" (Psalm 27:1 NIV). How did light in the darkness give you courage?

3. In which specific area of your life—circumstance, decision, or relationship—did you ask God to help you gain courage?

BEAUTY

1. Is there a specific place you go or a thing you do that really invites you to remember the beauty of the Lord?

2. How did focusing on the word *beauty* help guide those you love to seek "the unfading beauty of a gentle and quiet spirit" (1 Peter 3:4 NIV)?

3. Was there a distraction, voice, or thing in your life that you needed to cut off or remove in order to focus on the beauty Jesus talks about?

Dear Jesus, thank You for helping me to cultivate a fulfilling, fruitful life. Help me to trust You with what grows. You are the ultimate gardener. You illuminate our paths and bring light to all circumstances. You are our hope in the darkness; let us point others to You amid every circumstance. Thank You for being our Source of all courage and the One we can run to whenever we are afraid. Show us opportunities to walk in this courage, bold and secure in You. Continue to lend me Your eyes as I seek to find beauty in myself, others, and the world around me. Help me not reach for things that don't satisfy. A heart that follows You—that is beautiful. In Jesus' name, amen.

Freedom

Whoever looks intently into the perfect law that gives freedom, and continues in it—not forgetting what they have heard, but doing it—they will be blessed in what they do.
JAMES 1:25 NIV

When we think of freedom, we don't usually think of parameters, right?

Freedom equals wide open spaces and no boundaries—full rein to do whatever we want to do, go wherever we want to go, and make any decision we want to make, yes?

Recently I was dog-sitting and the dog ran away. Apparently he was old in age, but that was news to me, because he zoomed past me, and his little hind legs carried him streets away from his home. I panicked and immediately started running after the little guy. After I had exhausted my energy, I hopped into my car and searched, frantically praying that she would pop out and say "Got ya!" in dog language. Minutes felt like hours, and finally, after calling in my husband for backup, we found her. The relief and peace I felt when I saw her tail wagging is a feeling I will never forget. While she had temporarily enjoyed her outing, the fear and desire to be back home was easily seen in her eyes.

This made me think about how often we misdefine freedom, thinking that it is about a lack of instruction and boundaries. Sadie (the pup) became endangered the minute she decided to forgo the limits placed on her by those who love her. It was out of a desire for her to have the best, longest, fullest life possible that she was given the constraints of a fence. While she may have escaped due to her feeling shorted by the boundaries of her backyard, she ended up searching for home.

Isn't this just like us and Jesus? We often misinterpret His provision as withholding possibility, but really, He is protecting our future. He knows that sometimes what feels, looks, or seems good right now is not for our ultimate good. He knows that the only way we can experience true freedom is when we obey His instruction. His commands are never so that we miss out on adventure; they are what preserve our life for the ultimate adventure! Jesus wants us to live the most abundant life possible. Because we can trust His boundary lines, we can run wild and free in the places He calls us to, knowing that fulfillment is only found there.

FOCUS TIP: This week, when you feel stuck in a situation you can't seem to get out of, remember the word *freedom* and know that because of Jesus, you are free to be who you were meant to be.

You, my brothers and sisters, were called to be free. But do not use your freedom to indulge the flesh; rather, serve one another humbly in love.

GALATIANS 5:13 NIV

"I have the right to do anything," you say—but not everything is beneficial. "I have the right to do anything"—but I will not be mastered by anything.

I CORINTHIANS 6:12 NIV

To the Jews who had believed him, Jesus said, "If you hold to my teaching, you are really my disciples. Then you will know the truth, and the truth will set you free."

JOHN 8:31–32 NIV

Now the Lord is the Spirit, and where the Spirit of the Lord is, there is freedom.

II CORINTHIANS 3:17 NIV

▼

Jesus, in obeying You, I find freedom. Amen.

Renew

Set your minds on things that are above,
not on things that are on earth.

COLOSSIANS 3:2 ESV

The average person generates over 50,000 thoughts per day. With only 86,400 seconds in a day (28,800 of which should be spent sleeping), that means we only have 57,600 seconds to think these 50,000 thoughts— almost one thought per second. This also means that there is no way our minds do not feel like they are traveling on a never-ending roller coaster. The crazy thing about the mind is that we have the brainpower and foresight to understand cause and effect. We understand that when we allow something to fester in our mind, it will either propel us toward our destiny or push us toward a setback. However, we can also deceive ourselves into thinking that we do not have to take authority over our thoughts.

Because behavior is what we see, we often equate change to behavior modification. If we can just alter this behavior or quit this habit, then everything will be different, right? However, any significant and lasting change is always possible because of a renewed mind. When we stop treating our thoughts as though they are our customers and we are waiting on them, we can begin to nurture good thoughts and tell the other ones to hit the road—no conversation necessary. As we begin to realize that our thoughts don't "happen" to us, we take ownership over our thought life and can begin pursuing the mind of Christ. Whether it be in the music we listen to, the social media we engage in, the friends we choose, or the hobbies we pursue—we will choose what aligns with a mind that pleases God.

With the mind of Christ, we do not grow weary when the unexpected occurs because we trust what He is doing. We do not fear opposition because we know that He is fighting for us. We see the future as hopeful because we know that He is working out all things for our good and His glory. We see those around us as brothers and sisters, no longer competing, condemning, or comparing ourselves because we know that He gives us the gift of each other. And no matter our circumstances, we can remain in a posture of peace because He is in control.

Our thoughts *will* wander, but if we continue to realign our focus, remember His Word, and renew our mind, we will see the power of Christ at work. A mind set on Jesus is a mind that will change the whole world.

FOCUS TIP: This week, as you focus on the word *renew*, try to capture your negative thoughts and recalibrate your mind into thoughts of gratefulness and love.

"Who has understood the mind of the Lord so as to instruct him?" But we have the mind of Christ.

I CORINTHIANS 2:16 ESV

Do not be conformed to this world, but be transformed by the renewal of your mind, that by testing you may discern what is the will of God, what is good and acceptable and perfect.

ROMANS 12:2 ESV

Therefore, preparing your minds for action, and being sober-minded, set your hope fully on the grace that will be brought to you at the revelation of Jesus Christ.

I PETER 1:13 ESV

Finally, brothers, whatever is true, whatever is honorable, whatever is just, whatever is pure, whatever is lovely, whatever is commendable, if there is any excellence, if there is anything worthy of praise, think about these things.

PHILIPPIANS 4:8 ESV

Jesus, renew my mind and restore my thoughts. Amen.

Trust

Let the morning bring me word of Your unfailing love, for I have put my trust in You. Show me the way I should go, for to You I entrust my life.

PSALM 143:8 NIV

"All right ladies, suit up. Get ready for the adventure of your lives!" my camp counselor shouted. I tried to be excited, especially considering how I was always down for a new activity, but we had only been at camp for two days. The sky was cloudy, and I knew that putting on our bathing suits meant that we would be near water. My counselor had spent maybe twenty minutes with me by then, and all I could think was, "She barely knows me! I don't want her determining my next adventure!"

Wearily, I suited up and we hit the lake. We ended up having a pretty awesome adventure. Although sailing in pre-storm weather isn't ideal, I learned that my counselor was able to offer advice and helpful instruction. When the boat did capsize, she came quickly and all was okay. *Why was I worried?* I have asked myself in the years since, visualizing my ten-year-old panicked mind going in circles. And then I realized it was because I didn't have the chance to develop trust in the one who was leading me. I didn't know that she had sailed those waters for over eleven years, had her paramedic license, and really did care about my welfare. But once I began to trust her, my fear turned into excitement and I was actually able to enjoy the experience. For two weeks, as she led the way on hikes and rope courses and everything in between, I could barely sleep out of anticipation for what the next day held. If my counselor was picking it, I knew it would be worth it.

I wonder if maybe our holdup about our next adventure in our current lives is due to a lack of trust in the One we follow. Are we certain He has our best in mind? Can we trust that He has walked this way before? Does He know what to do if inclement weather occurs? Does He love me enough to stick with me even when I try to get ahead of His plan?

Oh, friends, there is no one on this planet who knows the kind of adventure our souls crave like our heavenly Father. He knows the best views to climb because He created it all. He knows what invigorates our souls and what calms our hearts; however, He will challenge us. He will instruct us to leap when we want to run, but we can rest assured that wherever He leads, it is for our best. The space between our comfort and our calling is what develops trust in our Creator. May we say yes to every adventure He offers, as every place is a stop on the road to abundant life.

FOCUS TIP: This week, every time you start worrying about what God has for your future, stop your anxious thoughts and, instead, whisper the word *trust*. Let God know you trust Him fully with whatever He has coming your way.

*Trust in the LORD with all your heart and lean not
on your own understanding; in all your ways submit
to Him, and He will make your paths straight.*
PROVERBS 3:5–6 NIV

When I am afraid, I put my trust in You.
PSALM 56:3 NIV

*He will not let your foot slip—He who
watches over you will not slumber.*
PSALM 121:3 NIV

*Blessed is the one who trusts in the LORD, whose confidence
is in Him. They will be like a tree planted by the water
that sends out its roots by the stream. It does not fear
when heat comes; its leaves are always green. It has no
worries in a year of drought and never fails to bear fruit.*
JEREMIAH 17:7–8 NIV

▼

*Jesus, lead the way.
I trust You. Amen.*

Anchored

This hope is a strong and trustworthy anchor for our souls.
It leads us through the curtain into God's inner sanctuary.
HEBREWS 6:19 NLT

*A*nchored. This word is so strong. The placement of our anchor reveals the place of our trust, hope, peace, strength, joy, compassion, and sustenance. What we tie ourselves to reveals what we believe can sustain us.

And when thinking about being anchored, we know that a boat must be anchored or it will drift. However, in our own lives, we forget that we tend to do the same. We hope our initial placement into the ground will be enough, not realizing that Sunday maintenance or casually following Jesus has never been enough of a stable foundation. We get sidetracked. We get busy striving. And suddenly we look up and think, *Wait, what is this place? How. Did. I. Get. Here?*

We get nowhere by accident. We drifted because we stopped being attentive to the origin of how we first set up camp in this place. The gratitude and the praise and the diligence and the prayer—it came easy at first. It was just what we did. But then we started doing other things, and we lost ourselves in them. We got really comfortable. And now we are frustrated. Our hearts feel hardened by what we see, and the palpable joy we experienced before has been overtaken by the gloom in front of us.

It's okay to be here. And if we are honest, we let ourselves drift pretty easily. The good news is that our true anchor—the grace of Jesus—never lost its way or its willingness to help us come back. When we dig ourselves into His truth and wrap our security around the certainty of His promises, we begin to feel that assurance once more. The sunshine starts to hit our faces and we see land . . . there it is. Okay, we're good.

Placing our security in finances, friendships, or future plans will always make us drift into waters that seem dependable at first but land us in disappointment. Our view has never been determined by what we have or where we've been or what our boat looks like, but about where we place our anchor—in what or whom we trust.

Our destination has never been a place, has it? Just a person. Jesus. However we word it, that's what we ultimately want to experience. Forever safety. When we are anchored in Him, He transforms our perspective, ushers peace in the storm, and provides eternal security. Is there a greater gift?

FOCUS TIP: When you find yourself with a differing opinion than your coworker, friend, or spouse this week, remember to think about the word *anchor* and make sure you are aligned with your Foundation. Then you can stand firm in your point of view. Just remember to ask God to steady you.

*Hope does not put us to shame, because God's
love has been poured out into our hearts through
the Holy Spirit, who has been given to us.*

ROMANS 5:5 NIV

*For God alone, O my soul, wait in silence, for
my hope is from him. He only is my rock and my
salvation, my fortress; I shall not be shaken.*

PSALM 62:5–6 ESV

*Let all who take refuge in You be glad; let them ever
sing for joy. Spread Your protection over them, that
those who love Your name may rejoice in You.*

PSALM 5:11 NIV

*We are pressed on every side by troubles, but we are
not crushed. We are perplexed, but not driven to despair.
We are hunted down, but never abandoned by God.
We get knocked down, but we are not destroyed.*

II CORINTHIANS 4:8–9 NLT

▼

*Jesus, anchored and sure,
I trust in You. Amen.*

▶ taking inventory:

FREEDOM

1. How did obeying Jesus increase the freedom in your life?

2. Did you notice how the boundaries He gave you are for your protection? When is a specific time this has been true for you?

3. Galatians says that we are to use our freedom to serve one another. How did this play out for you the week you focused on the word *freedom*?

RENEW

1. Paul tells the Philippians to think about things that are true, honorable, just, pure, lovely, recommendable, excellent, and worthy of praise. Which attributes did you work on most when focusing on the word *renew*?

2. In what ways did you ask Jesus to renew your mind?

3. After focusing on *renew*, do you now have a better understanding of the importance of taking your thoughts captive?

TRUST

1. What adventures did God reveal to you? Are you trusting Him in this new season?

2. Did you find it difficult to "lean not on your own understanding" (Proverbs 3:5 NIV)? Or easy?

3. Is there a time God proved His trustworthiness to you?

ANCHORED

1. Have you ever drifted from your anchor? What have you done to reset it?

2. Is someone in your life drifting? Are you helping them realign?

3. When focused on the word *anchored*, did you find that you were putting your trust in someone or something that wasn't solid?

Dear Jesus, thank You for being the protector of my freedom and my life. You want me to enjoy new adventures, and I'm so grateful for that. Help me to focus on life-giving things, Jesus. When my thoughts begin to wander, renew my mind and lead me back to You. Thank You for graciously leading me in all moments. Will You help me trust Your ways, even when I don't understand them?

God, You are dependable and sure; help me anchor myself in You so that I will not be tossed by the waves of life. Remind my heart that Your Word is my foundation and my future is secure in You. In Jesus' name, amen.

Expect

It was by faith that Moses left the land of Egypt, not fearing the king's anger. He kept right on going because he kept his eyes on the One who is invisible.

HEBREWS 11:27 NLT

There is a big difference between expectation and comprehension, though we tend to link the two sometimes, believing one to naturally come with the other. We think that in order to expect Jesus to work, we must fully comprehend the specifics of *how* He will work. We struggle with crafting expectations because we seek to fully understand His ways first.

Many times, we set our expectations based on our desires rather than on His given instruction from His Word. We have a preconceived idea of what faithfulness should look like in our situations, and even though we are aware that He is God and we are not, our trust becomes built on whether He met or exceeded our expectations. We become resentful with unanswered prayers, frustrated with His timing, and confused by His definition of provision.

However, if we dug into Scripture, we would see that Jesus has long anticipated us to be confused by how He works and when He works. He assured us that His ways are higher than our ways and His timeline will often not match up to ours. His ability to deliver or exceed our expectations has never been up for question; it has always been our lack of trust based on our small expectations that has limited our potential.

The God of the Bible gave Sarah a baby at the ripe age of ninety. He delivered Jonah from the mouth of a whale. He protected Daniel in the lion's den. He gave Esther the courage to save an entire people. He performed miracle after miracle after miracle. If we truly believed in that same God to show up in our lives and we set our expectations on His shoulders, what would change for us? If we really thought the God of the universe was going to meet us in our quiet time, we would probably prioritize it, right?

Many times we interchange *expect* with *wish* and our hope is loose, as shifty as the ocean waves. But when we expect something, we operate in confidence and certainty. When we expect God to show up, we lean on it, plan for it, and live in a way as if it has already happened.

How do we know what to expect? We read His Word. We educate ourselves and inform our heart of His promises, we ask for the faith to believe them, and then we step forward in anticipation. Expectations make God's voice the loudest in our lives, letting the foundation of His character form the way we embrace the present, past, and future.

FOCUS TIP: As you focus on *expect* this week, think big. God performs miracles. Ask Him for the faith to believe and then *expect* Him to show up.

*The hope of the righteous brings joy, but the
expectation of the wicked will perish.*
PROVERBS 10:28 ESV

*God is able to make all grace abound to you,
so that having all sufficiency in all things at all
times, you may abound in every good work.*
II CORINTHIANS 9:8 ESV

*Now to Him who is able to do far more
abundantly than all that we ask or think,
according to the power at work within us . . .*
EPHESIANS 3:20 ESV

*He said to them, "Because of your little faith. For truly, I
say to you, if you have faith like a grain of mustard seed,
you will say to this mountain, 'Move from here to there,'
and it will move, and nothing will be impossible for you."*
MATTHEW 17:20 ESV

▼

*Jesus, I live expectantly,
because You're at work. Amen.*

Create

According to the grace of God given to me, like a skilled master builder I laid a foundation, and someone else is building upon it. Let each one take care how he builds upon it.

I CORINTHIANS 3:10 ESV

Have you ever thought about the way the ocean waves roll in, the way the stars align to light up the entire sky, or how the systems of nature all work together to create this beautiful place we call home? The very beginning of the Bible starts with, "In the beginning God created the heavens and the earth" (Genesis 1:1). Isn't it overwhelming and beyond magnificent that our God established creation? There was no thought of ocean, stars, or systems before He made them to be.

Genesis 1:26 then goes on to say that God created mankind "in His image." This means that whatever qualities God embodies, so does man. If God is creative, then so are we. We are all molded with a unique makeup—consisting of God-given gifts, passions, mindset, and heart. It is this powerful combination that works together to form what we can offer back to God—our service.

When was the last time you created something? Whether it be painting a picture, writing an article, decorating a room, or putting together a PowerPoint presentation, there are infinite ways in which we can exercise this creative gene. Unlike a lot of things, we are not working with a limited supply. Because we were built by the God of the universe, the more we use our creativity, the more we find we have. As our confidence grows and we find freedom in our strokes, we realize that the creation process was far less about the outcome and more about the person we become while making our masterpiece. Just like Jesus, we find beauty, hope, and joy in the things we give our hands to because they point to our heavenly Father above all.

We are known to short-circuit ourselves, dumbing down what we do out of fear of rejection or failure. But how is it possible to do something that has never been done before in the wrong way? That is the beauty of creativity!

He is only interested in your contribution done in your creative way—giving your all as an act of worship to the One who made you.

Go on—create. You can't do it wrong! How freeing is that?

FOCUS TIP: This week, have fun connecting your faith with your creativity. You can hand-letter a Scripture, paint a picture of your favorite nature scene, or write your very own devotional. And talk to God throughout the process, letting your creative juices flow and growing in your connection with your heavenly Father.

We are his workmanship, created in Christ Jesus for good works, which God prepared beforehand, that we should walk in them.
EPHESIANS 2:10 ESV

But now, O LORD, You are our Father, we are the clay, and You our potter; and all of us are the work of Your hand.
ISAIAH 64:8 NASB

Having gifts that differ according to the grace given to us, let us use them: if prophecy, in proportion to our faith; if service, in our serving; the one who teaches, in his teaching; the one who exhorts, in his exhortation; the one who contributes, in generosity; the one who leads, with zeal; the one who does acts of mercy, with cheerfulness.
ROMANS 12:6–8 ESV

Do not neglect the gift you have, which was given you by prophecy when the council of elders laid their hands on you.
I TIMOTHY 4:14 ESV

*Jesus, I choose to create,
as I worship the Creator. Amen.*

Purpose

Go therefore and make disciples of all nations, baptizing them in the name of the Father and of the Son and of the Holy Spirit, teaching them to observe all that I have commanded you.

MATTHEW 28:19–20 ESV

Somehow we have convinced ourselves that our purpose is unknown; we have believed the lie that once we graduate from college or high school and become an adult, we must set sail and discover why we were created. However, if we believe that Jesus is real and His Word is true, His purpose for our lives is anything but confusing.

Time and time again, He tells us that we are here to make disciples. We are meant to bring heaven to earth, to tell others about the love of Jesus, and to serve selflessly and sacrificially. Our purpose is essentially pointing to Him in whatever we do, whatever we say, and however we live. The purpose of our lives is manifested through unique callings, yes. However, one does not have to travel as a missionary, work at a church, or write a Christian book to be considered "in ministry." When we realize that the purpose of our lives is to be disciples who make disciples, we assume the authority that we are all in ministry, just in different ways. Whether it be coaching a baseball team, performing in a band, or working the register at Panera, we have the privilege to begin every day with the same mindset: how can I give of myself so that He can be known?

The point of our lives is not to speak the language to everyone who already knows it—impressing those around us with how far we have come or what we have done. It is the extension of our hands, the willingness of our feet, and the softness of our heart toward those who don't know Jesus that pleases Him.

Though the particulars of our path may seem confusing at times, His purpose for us is clear. We will face opposition, but His purpose for us is sure. And we will get discouraged, but His purpose for us is not up for negotiation. As we share about His love and tell others of His grace, we will experience a fulfillment that far outweighs any outcome we can see. Our spirit was meant to boast in the One who made us, growing His family and bringing heaven to earth.

FOCUS TIP: Do you ever wonder why you are where you are in life? This week, be reminded that you are here, on this earth, at this moment in time, for a specific purpose—to love God and others. This week, try to make this your only goal and see how God shows up.

The Lord will fulfill his purpose for me; your steadfast love, O Lord, endures forever. Do not forsake the work of your hands.

PSALM 138:8 ESV

Before I formed you in the womb I knew you, and before you were born I consecrated you; I appointed you a prophet to the nations.

JEREMIAH 1:5 ESV

Worthy are you, our Lord and God, to receive glory and honor and power, for you created all things, and by your will they existed and were created.

REVELATION 4:11 ESV

For this purpose I have raised you up, to show you my power, so that my name may be proclaimed in all the earth.

EXODUS 9:16 ESV

▼

Jesus, making disciples, purposed for You. Amen.

Intentionality

*Look carefully then how you walk, not as unwise
but as wise, making the best use of the time, because
the days are evil. Therefore, do not be foolish, but
understand what the will of the Lord is.*

EPHESIANS 5:15–17 ESV

We all have really good intentions. We get in these moods and we are ready to conquer the world, right? This is it—now is the time we are going to be better about reaching out to that friend, more consistent in our quiet time, persistent in our workouts, or available to serve in that organization.

And then suddenly the days pile up and the months pass by, and we are rounding the corner again, frustrated that nothing has changed. Our intentions were there but we never did anything with them, only leading to more guilt and shame that we just can't seem to get it together.

How do we become more intentional with our lives? The mistake so many of us make is that we are waiting to feel something before we do something. We pray that the desire comes and then the deliverance will happen, but more often than not, we do not wake up inviting change.

Implementing any type of change requires that we travel outside our comfort zones and dip our toes into the unknown or unfamiliar, and that is not something we will do on a whim.

However, I have seen the power of scheduling and signing up to get uncomfortable. Maybe it's that small group that you sign up for and purchase the book for, and now others are expecting you to come. Or maybe it's attending a workout class that you prepay, knowing that if you enter your credit card information, your feet will show up, even if it's begrudgingly. Maybe it's that conversation with your spouse where you keep saying, "We really need to be better about fruitful conversation," but it never happens. So you both schedule time once a week to check in and offer more than the normal small talk.

If we are going to get serious about being intentional, we are going to have to block out time in our schedule, even when it feels like life is too full.

Chances are, adding something that matters to your regimen will force you to remove something that doesn't. This step of obedience will remove pressure from your shoulders and allow the margin to live a more intentional life.

And when we struggle with what to add and subtract, we can pray. Jesus honors a heart that is desiring to be available to Him. He will help us, but we must be participants in order to add action steps.

Make time for what matters to Jesus. Rest in this truth: no one ever looks back and regrets how intentionally they lived; however, many reflect and wish they could have given their time to things that last in eternity. Building a legacy begins now.

FOCUS TIP: What are two things you have been intending to do for months? Can you do them this week?

Above all, my brothers, do not swear, either by heaven or by earth or by any other oath, but let your "yes" be yes and your "no" be no, so that you may not fall under condemnation.

JAMES 5:12 ESV

Walk in wisdom toward outsiders, making the best use of the time.

COLOSSIANS 4:5 ESV

I know, O LORD, that the way of man is not in himself, that it is not in man who walks to direct his steps.

JEREMIAH 10:23 ESV

You shall love the Lord your God with all your heart, with all your soul, and with all your strength.

DEUTERONOMY 6:5 NKJV

▼

Jesus, I'm setting my intentions, and following through. Amen.

▶ taking inventory:

EXPECT

1. How did God show up for you?

2. After focusing on the word *expect*, do you feel as if your expectations are more linked to your faith?

3. Did you learn to live in expectation of a miracle-working God?

CREATE

1. How did connecting your creativity with your faith help you deepen your relationship with Christ?

2. By focusing on the word *create*, did you think about how God created you to be one-of-a-kind?

3. How can you make all the things you create (dinner, friendships, study groups, paintings, etc.) acts of worship?

PURPOSE

1. Were you able to focus on living into your purpose while maintaining all your other roles?

2. Has God shown you His power in your life? How can you proclaim that to others?

3. Did focusing on the word *purpose* help you believe that God has purpose in everything He does and all He creates?

INTENTIONALITY

1. What two things were you intentional about doing this past week?

2. What did you release from your routine schedule? What did you add?

3. Do you know anyone who is intentional with their time and energy? Have you thanked them for being such a great example?

*Dear Jesus, thank You for being
faithful and constant. Help me to
build my expectations based on Your
Word and live in a way that says I
know You are worthy of my trust.
Your gift of creativity is truly amazing.
You made the heavens and earth, and
then You made me. Thank You for helping
me tap into Your creative juices to find a
new way to worship. I love You, Jesus.
Thank You for being the King of
intentionality, always guiding us in
how to show up well for ourselves and
others. Help us release what doesn't
matter and make time for what does.
Thank You for establishing my purpose
long ago. My life is significant because it
points to You. Help me to be bold as I live
for You. There is no greater purpose.
In Jesus' name, amen.*

Surrender

He said to me, "My grace is sufficient for you, for my power is made perfect in weakness." Therefore I will boast all the more gladly of my weaknesses, so that the power of Christ may rest upon me."

II CORINTHIANS 12:9 ESV

When we think of surrendering, we automatically think of losing, right?

When wrestlers tap out and surrender, they lose the match. When an army raises the white flag and surrenders, they lose the battle. Having the knowledge of what these two examples insinuate, when Jesus tells us to "surrender," it is so difficult for our brains to recognize that His instruction is not equivalent to joining the losing team.

The hard part about raising the white flag is that it requires us to fully admit that we are not in control. Though we like to deceive ourselves into thinking so, we are not the one who holds that kind of power. We often fight tooth and nail until we are exhausted, on the mat sweating, and finally decide it's time—if we don't tap out, we won't make it. We will be overpowered.

But like so many things in the kingdom of God, surrender has never been synonymous with defeat. It is precisely the way we enter into victory. The moment that we realize we can't fight alone, we link arms with the mountain-mover and Creator of the world. As He works wonders, gives guidance to our steps, and helps us learn how to fight our enemy, we see that He has been in control the entire time. He was simply waiting on us to release—to let go—to trust that His plans for our lives do not end the second we surrender; rather, they begin.

If we know this is true, why is it that we often white-knuckle our way into the ground, refusing to give Him what He already owns? Often it's a fear that what we have is not enough. This insecurity develops an odd sense of pride in our heart, being selfish with our energy and our gifts. Or we begin to second-guess His goodness toward us. *Does He really have my best in mind? Maybe I should withhold a little bit, just in case*, we think. This shortsighted view of self-preservation actually leads to self-sabotage, as the very piece we hold onto becomes the foothold keeping us from freedom.

Surrender is the only pathway to peace, joy, and trans-formation. When we steward what we have well by giving it to Him, we take the pressure off ourselves to perform the miracle, and we trust that He will. And ten times out of ten, He is on the winning team. The safest place for anything valuable, including ourselves, is only found in the hands of the King.

FOCUS TIP: As you focus on *surrender* this week, remember to raise the white flag when your pride sets in. Remind yourself to release it all to God.

*Submit yourselves therefore to God. Resist
the devil, and he will flee from you.*
JAMES 4:7 ESV

*And he said, "Abba, Father, all things are
possible for you. Remove this cup from me.
Yet not what I will, but what you will."*
MARK 14:36 ESV

*My son, give me your heart, and let
your eyes observe my ways.*
PROVERBS 23:26 ESV

*I have been crucified with Christ. It is no longer I
who live, but Christ who lives in me. And the life
I now live in the flesh I live by faith in the Son of
God, who loved me and gave himself for me.*
GALATIANS 2:20 ESV

▼

*Jesus, in my surrender,
I find my victory. Amen.*

Words

Let the words of my mouth and the meditation of my heart be acceptable in your sight, O Lord, my rock and my redeemer.

PSALM 19:14 ESV

Words—a daily, integral, large part of every person's existence, no matter where they live, what they do, their personality, or what they dream for their lives.

At almost every moment, other than those few when we find the discipline and peace to be truly silent in ourselves, we are talking. We are sharing words with others, typing words on our phones, hearing words on the radio, or speaking words within the confines of our own minds. And even in our silence, we are receiving words spoken over and to us from the Lord. That means that at every moment, words are impacting our lives in some capacity.

I believe it would be a pretty interesting study if we were able to generate a spreadsheet or some type of data-gathering system that populated the words of all different kinds of people and then assimilated those into groupings. Would we find commonalities among those who live in certain places or perform specific jobs? What about our backgrounds and our current environments: how much do those impact our words? And what about the input systems we tap into, such as music, television, and literature: how much does what we hear transform the way we think and, in turn, the words we see ourselves? Such a study, obviously complex in nature, would probably reveal some patterns that would blow our minds.

Knowing how much the different inputs we allow affect the output we deliver, how can we be more aware? With so many choices and such saturation of words, is there something that can help us navigate this and choose what is beneficial for our lives? Yes. Even for those who don't believe, the Word of God is the only Word that is alive and active. When we choose to dig into the pages of Scripture, we are deciding to fill our heart and mind with truth and light. The Bible was always meant to be the manual for the words we receive and those we release. Though we cannot control the mouths of others, we do have authority over the way they influence our lives. We must be the gatekeeper over our heart, realizing that even the seemingly unimportant social media posts or texts from a friend can penetrate our heart and affect our future.

Our words have the power to defeat the enemy, speak life into dry bones, bring confidence into hopeless situations, and turn on the lights when the room feels dark. Just as toothpaste can't be squeezed back into the tube, words cannot be unsaid or unheard. Let's speak life over ourselves, absorb ourselves into the living Word, and place ourselves in life-giving atmospheres. Words matter in every space we sit.

FOCUS TIP: This week, before you speak, think through the words you use. Take note of the words people speak to you— and decide whether or not to let them into your heart. Discard the ones that don't speak truth and love.

The words of the reckless pierce like swords,
but the tongue of the wise brings healing.
PROVERBS 12:18 NIV

Gracious words are a honeycomb, sweet to
the soul and healing to the bones.
PROVERBS 16:24 NIV

It's not what goes into your mouth that defiles you; you
are defiled by the words that come out of your mouth.
MATTHEW 15:11 NLT

Do not let any unwholesome talk come out of your mouths,
but only what is helpful for building others up according
to their needs, that it may benefit those who listen.
EPHESIANS 4:29 NIV

Jesus, help my words to
reflect Your Word. Amen.

Simplicity

God is not a God of confusion but of peace.

I CORINTHIANS 14:33 ESV

Stuff takes up our space. Commitments require our time. Investments demand our energy. However, if anyone looked at our lives from a bird's-eye view based on the stuff we have, the commitments we sign up for, and the investments we make, they would assume we have an unlimited supply of both time and energy.

We find ourselves begging for more margin in our lives but we aren't willing to give the discipline or intentionality it takes to create it. In order for us to experience that deep breath and have the space we crave, we must simplify our lives so that we can begin to see clearly again.

Tangibly, this looks like decluttering our home, our car, our office, and other spaces we inhabit. When we try to operate in a space that is chaotic, we naturally become poor stewards of the things we have. Our lives feel like a constant game of hide-and-seek and our hearts feel the frustration, guilt, and impatience that accompanies it.

Spiritually, this practice resembles finding our rhythm and establishing spiritual disciplines within this rhythm that keep us accountable to pursuing the Lord without feeling overwhelmed or defeated. These rhythms include tending to our space, our commitments, our workflow, and anything that takes up space in our minds.

Relationally, this translates to being intentional with our time and our schedules. When we stop trying to be relevant everywhere, we allow ourselves to be effective and helpful somewhere.

Think about Jesus. He was a simple man. He did not feel the need to be all places at once. He had twelve disciples, even though thousands flocked to Him. He was not the most wealthy or seemingly "important" man according to the societal standards at the time. However, it was His attentiveness to His father—His awareness of what was most important—that marked His life. It was actually the simplicity of His life that allowed His message to be even clearer.

And overall, these ways of somewhat decluttering all around us allow us to pursue transformation within us. When we stop distracting ourselves with things to tend to, fix, or maintain, we give ourselves space to know what we actually enjoy. And God's kindness becomes obvious in our lives.

Addressing the mess around us allows us to sit down with Jesus as He addresses the mess within us.

Simplifying our lives isn't about taking the easy route. It's about removing some of the unnecessary choices we make daily so that we can more consistently choose things that glorify Him. The gospel is simple; may our everyday rhythms reflect that.

FOCUS TIP: This week, focus on simplifying your life. Before starting a task or signing up to volunteer at that event, think about your word—*simplicity*—and ask God whether He wants you to add more to your schedule or if He wants your time spent elsewhere.

Don't wear yourself out trying to get rich; restrain yourself! Riches disappear in the blink of an eye; wealth sprouts wings and flies off into the wild blue yonder.
PROVERBS 23:4 THE MESSAGE

True godliness with contentment is itself great wealth. After all, we brought nothing with us when we came into the world, and we can't take anything with us when we leave it.
I TIMOTHY 6:6–7 NLT

Create in me a clean heart, O God, and renew a right spirit within me.
PSALM 51:10 ESV

Do your best to present yourself to God as one approved, a worker who has no need to be ashamed, rightly handling the word of truth.
II TIMOTHY 2:15 ESV

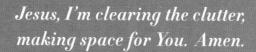

Jesus, I'm clearing the clutter, making space for You. Amen.

Obedience

Whoever looks intently into the perfect law that gives freedom, and continues in it—not forgetting what they have heard, but doing it—they will be blessed in what they do.

JAMES 1:25 NIV

We grow up hearing "obey your parents," "obey your teachers," and many other phrases we've stamped as typical. These phrases were instructed of us usually to avoid punishment, knowing that consequences followed our disobedience. And so our mindset was created of this word obedience—a word that often triggers the thought in our head: *avoid punishment*.

This mindset we have crafted causes us to focus more on the action/command and less on the Giver of it. If we think God is unfair, arrogant, or unaware of our human needs, why would we listen to what He has to say? If we think He withholds good from us, will we put our trust in His ways? Probably not. Our human desire to find fulfillment will claw its way forward, pushing us to pursue what might satisfy and believing that it might be outside of what God knows, wants, provides, or instructs.

So maybe we should ask ourselves, based on our past experiences, have we ever regretted following Him? When we have experienced discomfort or heartache, has He ever failed to provide us with what we need to navigate life's unexpected moments? No. Never. His presence has always been our comfort. Even when we betray or reject Him, His character remains consistent. The hard part is that obedience continually requires us to deny ourselves and what we visibly see. It asks us to forgo our pride and self-preservation and to trust the heart of our Father. Obedience asks us to base our perspective on His promise and trust His process to arrive there. And when we do? Our eyes are opened to what He is doing, solidifying our hope that He has been at work the whole time, working in the invisible places that provide lasting transformation.

If we surveyed our own lives—our habits, our tendencies, our choices, and our relationships—would we find a correlation between emptiness and disobedience? Could it be that we are still pursuing pain and hoping something changes? Wherever we struggle to follow Him reveals where we are hesitant to trust Him. Our behavior is what's on the surface, but it's our heart He is after. He is yearning for us to fear and obey Him so that we can actually experience true life. God never asks for our obedience to hold us back; He commands it because He wants us to run forth. Because He made us, He knows what satisfies us and what drains us. And that if we follow Him, His unwavering faithfulness will remind us that the narrow way is worth the sacrifice.

FOCUS TIP: As you focus on *obedience* this week, think through all the kindness, all the love, all the care, all the forgiveness that Jesus has freely given you. Being obedient isn't hard—it's a response to the love He wraps us in daily.

He replied, "Blessed rather are those who
hear the word of God and obey it."

LUKE 11:28 NIV

This is the love of God, that we keep his commandments.
And his commandments are not burdensome.

I JOHN 5:3 ESV

Praise the Lord! Blessed is the man who fears the
Lord, who greatly delights in his commandments!

PSALM 112:1 ESV

The end of the matter; all has been heard. Fear God and
keep his commandments, for this is the whole duty of man.

ECCLESIASTES 12:13 ESV

▼

*Jesus, help me to obey You
and trust Your heart. Amen.*

▶ taking inventory:

SURRENDER

1. What were you led to surrender?

2. Did focusing on the word *surrender* lead you to peace, joy, and transformation in your life?

3. Is there a specific situation, relationship, or thing you still might need to surrender at His feet?

WORDS

1. Most words we are say are either to impress others or control others. If that insight rings true to you, how can you guard against those intended words?

2. Think about a person whose words uplift you. Were you able to follow their example?

3. What words did you say to yourself? Do they align with the words God says about you?

SIMPLICITY

1. Are you "wearing yourself out to get rich" or maybe even just to make ends meet in your current circumstances? How did focusing on *simplicity* help you?

2. What two steps did you take to simplify or declutter your surroundings?

3. Do you resonate with the phrase "less is more"? In what areas of your life have you applied this truth?

OBEDIENCE

1. Did you find the connection between obedience and trust?

2. Were you able to obey God by doing something you were avoiding? What was the outcome?

3. Is there a time when your desires didn't match what God was asking of you but you obeyed and experienced the peace He promises?

*Dear Jesus, thank You for helping
me raise the white flag even when my
stubbornness and pride fight against
it. Remind my heart that whatever I
release to You will be in good hands.
Sometimes I find it hard to choose words
that align with Your Word. Give me wisdom
as I pick my words and also discernment
as I let those from others impact my soul.
Thank You for showing me how to
pursue simplicity in all facets of my
life. Show me what matters and help
me clear all other clutter away.
You are trustworthy and faithful.
Thank You for loving me! Please help
me respond to that great love with my
obedience, especially when I am tempted
to choose what's easy or popular. I
want to live a life that pleases You.
In Jesus' name, amen.*

With

. . . Teaching them to observe all that I have commanded you.
And behold, I am with you always, to the end of the age.

MATTHEW 28:20 ESV

It seems as though we have told ourselves that the minute we feel tension, opposition, or uncertainty, we must run. Onto the next. This space is hard. Surely all would go smoothly if we were in sync with Jesus, right? But that's never been His promise. In fact, He assures us of the opposite: we will face trouble. However, He also promises this: when we do, He is with us.

We tend to forget this truth, extending our hands once again for temporary comfort and false control, all to realize that our fortitude is never built in those spaces, comfort has never been our calling, and control has never been ours.

And then we ask, "Lord, can you move this out of my way? Are you aware that this isn't what I signed up for?"

And He knows. Oh, doesn't He always! He is fully aware that our frustration level is high and our discouragement is setting in, and He gently whispers, "Hey, you . . . look up. Don't be so surprised by the hard. We will do it together. Here [as He puts His hands out], empty your concerns into My hands. None are too small or too heavy. And pick up this peace, will you? Nothing must change for you to hold it in your heart. Remember, this is not your home. But in the in-between, as I know you want to run, will you run to Me? Your faith is growing.

"I see you've stopped leaning on your old safety net and you're pressing in—that's my hope. Ask me for what You need. You aren't too much. Patience? A little more trust? Increased awareness of My hand at work? I'll provide. Your nearness is where life is found."

And this place, the one we wanted to leave? We begin to crave the security it offers. His character proves to be true and trustworthy, our body stops being so tossed by the waves, and our mind begins to realign with truth.

As our feet move forward in the direction we wanted to detour, we find unexplainable joy and heavenly comfort. He reinvigorates our passion, reclaims our focus, and restores our grit.

Because He is with us, we know that when we feel rejected, He affirms us. When we feel unsteady, He is unshakable. When we feel fearful, He will help us.

It is actually in this space precisely—the one we never pick—that we understand the source of our peace. This place of dependence required our surrender, and in that our hearts actually grasped what it means to be safe.

FOCUS TIP: When fear overcomes you this week, remember *with*—God is *with* you. You are not alone. He will never forsake you. Know it, believe it, stand on it.

Fear not, for I am with you; be not dismayed, for I am your God; I will strengthen you, I will help you, I will uphold you with my righteous right hand.
ISAIAH 41:10 ESV

Now go! I will be with you as you speak, and I will instruct you in what to say.
EXODUS 4:12 NLT

The LORD your God is going with you! He will fight for you against your enemies, and He will give you victory!
DEUTERONOMY 20:4 NLT

No one will be able to stand against you as long as you live. For I will be with you as I was with Moses. I will not fail you or abandon you.
JOSHUA 1:5 NLT

Jesus, wherever I go,
You are with me. Amen.

Family

Love one another with brotherly affection.
Outdo one another in showing honor.

ROMANS 12:10 ESV

When we hear the word "family," we usually think of those closest to us. It may not always be those we are connected with through blood, but rather through relationship. Family connotes an intimacy present that is not just your usual relationship; it signifies importance and meaning. We often have our "work family," our "school family," our "church family," our "family family," our "gym family," and our "friend family." Most of these relationships are cultivated through convenience due to proximity, unifying habits and tendencies or relationships ignited by desire. There is an element of control that we seek to implement into these spaces, allowing our comfort zone to determine our reach.

But what does Jesus say about family? Have you looked? In Mark 3, Jesus addresses a crowd of people discussing His family and says, "Whoever does God's will is my brother and sister and mother" (v. 35 NIV). It is not that His family ties meant nothing to Him; rather, it was that His Father's definition of family defined everything for Him. The goal of Jesus was never exclusivity or assumption; He radically pursued all types of people in hopes of extending His family and building the kingdom. His only parameter was that they sought the will of God. In other words, He asked, "Are you looking to follow My Father?" and if the answer was yes, then family they became. And therefore anyone who was not in His family, Jesus sought to extend the greatest love to them. His goal was always to extend the family of His Father, and He knew the only method was offering love and lavish grace to those who felt alone.

How different would our lives look if we went on a bubble-destroying mission in our own lives? What would happen if we responded in immediacy, forgave quickly, and fought for the potential of others like we do for our earthly families? Are there people whom we treat differently because they don't fit inside the compartments we have created? If we offer empathy and kindness to those in our "church family," why don't those in our "work family" receive the same? If our standards waver based on those we are interacting with, we have forgotten who we are imitating. Jesus chose to intently see, love, and serve all. He crafted no assumptions and exerted no preferences.

May we take this same family approach, allowing only one thing to determine how we love: "Are you looking to follow my Father?" If yes, they are family. And if not, may we love them so they know what true family really, truly looks like.

FOCUS TIP: While focusing on *family* this week, try to redefine the term in your head. Your *family* may be the struggling mom in the grocery store with three rowdy kids. Look for times you can encourage and support the *family* around you.

*This is my commandment, that you love one another
as I have loved you. Greater love has no one than
this, that someone lay down his life for his friends.*
JOHN 15:12–13 ESV

*So then, as we have opportunity, let us do good to everyone,
and especially to those who are of the household of faith.*
GALATIANS 6:10 ESV

*I appeal to you, brothers, by the name of our Lord
Jesus Christ, that all of you agree, and that there
be no divisions among you, but that you be united
in the same mind and the same judgment.*
I CORINTHIANS 1:10 ESV

*Therefore, having put away falsehood, let each
one of you speak the truth with his neighbor,
for we are members one of another.*
EPHESIANS 4:25 ESV

▼

*Jesus, we are here to extend,
never exclude. Amen.*

Wait

*The LORD is good to those who wait
for him, to the soul who seeks him.*
LAMENTATIONS 3:25 ESV

Have you ever found yourself in the midst of a storm and thought, *Where is Jesus? Based on the promises He's given, how could He let me go through this?*

Frustrated with how different our current view is from our expected destination, we find ourselves questioning His goodness. We find our faith wavering, not even realizing that once again we have confined Him to our human box. We expect His presence to manifest itself in a certain way and His provision to answer our questions, our prayers, and our uncertainties in a particular manner and most definitely on our time line.

But He knows that the greatest miracle will not be the deliverance from the storm or the answer to our burning questions or the promise that we feel is far away. Rather, it's when our heart trusts in Him, when we develop heavenly patience that believes His time line is worth believing in, seeking, and waiting for.

The revelation made possible only because of the wait that makes us ripe for His work. It gives us freedom from what we see because we know that His presence is within us. And that He is near. And that whenever we find ourselves wanting to watch the clock tick or get anxious about the fact that we are still rowing in a sea that seems to be getting more powerful, we can go back to this truth: He doesn't just walk on water to come to us; He can make us arrive at *any* destination in a moment's time. Our schedules, expectations, or predicted boxes cannot confine our King.

Let's be honest—if Jesus were like a driving service and He arrived when we wanted, was driving exactly what we thought He was going to be driving, and always took us where we wanted to go, we would give orders and live a life that required very little faith.

The miracle is in the waiting. This battle—the one between the fear of what our eyes see and the waves that roar ahead versus the truth of what we know and what we claim to believe—it is hard-pressed and necessary.

Because in the exhaustion of our rowing and the desperation for deliverance, we experience a longing for our Savior. And when He comes, in His perfect timing and sovereign way, we remember that, once again, He is exactly who He says He is.

Our miracle was never in arriving at the shoreline but in trusting and believing that He could get us there.

FOCUS TIP: This week, trust Jesus to show you how to wait in wisdom and grace. Use the verse "Be still and know" to remind you that He is God and you're not.

But as for me, I will look to the L<small>ORD</small>; I will wait for the God of my salvation; my God will hear me.
MICAH 7:7 ESV

Behold, we consider those blessed who remained steadfast. You have heard of the steadfastness of Job, and you have seen the purpose of the Lord, how the Lord is compassionate and merciful.
JAMES 5:11 ESV

For still the vision awaits its appointed time; it hastens to the end—it will not lie. If it seems slow, wait for it; it will surely come; it will not delay.
HABAKKUK 2:3 ESV

I believe that I shall look upon the goodness of the L<small>ORD</small> in the land of the living! Wait for the L<small>ORD</small>; be strong, and let your heart take courage; wait for the L<small>ORD</small>!
PSALM 27:13–14 ESV

▼

*Jesus, in the wait,
I learn who You are. Amen.*

Jesus

The members of the council were amazed when they saw the boldness of Peter and John, for they could see that they were ordinary men with no special training in the Scriptures. They also recognized them as men who had been with Jesus.

ACTS 4:13 NLT

Have you heard about the story of Peter and John healing the lame beggar in Acts 3? It's an incredible story. Essentially, there was a lame man who had been crippled since birth. As Peter and John are on their way to prayer service at the temple, they see this man and stop. Paul responds to the man's begging and says, "I don't have any silver or gold for you. But I'll give you what I have. In the name of Jesus Christ the Nazarene, get up and walk!" (Acts 3:6 NLT). Peter extends his hand and the man is instantly healed, shocking every eye watching that day. As the council questioned them and they continued to give all praise to God, the council responded to their boldness by saying that they realized these men were ordinary but the difference was, they had "been with Jesus" (Acts 4:13 NLT).

That was Peter and John's secret sauce and the enemy's kryptonite: the power of the living God was at work. This story makes me wonder: Do our lives look like we have been with Jesus? Does our mindset resemble someone who has spent time in His Word? Does our boldness originate in the confidence of our Father? Do we think, speak, and act differently because we know Him and because we are loved by Him?

Sure, we are ordinary, but when we partner with the extraordinary—the same Jesus who rolled the stone away and rose on the third day—we get to take part in miracles. For some reason, we tend to let the culture that surrounds us and the voices of others tell us what is radical. What would others think if we pulled a Peter and stopped on the side of the road, extended our hand, and believed for total healing for another? Perhaps we are called to be exactly what we often fear—radical. Perhaps our faith out loud will be what prompts another to ask, "Who is this Jesus guy?"

He is the name above all names and the only one capable of saving our souls. He empowers us through His Word, positions us with His hand, and ushers peace through His heart. May our lives be full of boldness, grace, and truth as we let the extraordinary meet our ordinary. May others look at us and know that we have been with Jesus.

FOCUS TIP: This week, whisper the name *Jesus* as you stumble onto circumstances that seem out of your hands—and then watch as He creates miracle after miracle.

If you abide in me, and my words abide in you, ask whatever you wish, and it will be done for you.
JOHN 15:7 ESV

Blessed are the pure in heart, for they shall see God.
MATTHEW 5:8 ESV

You will receive power when the Holy Spirit has come upon you, and you will be my witnesses in Jerusalem and in all Judea and Samaria, and to the end of the earth.
ACTS 1:8 ESV

He was crucified in weakness, but lives by the power of God. For we also are weak in him, but in dealing with you we will live with him by the power of God.
II CORINTHIANS 13:4 ESV

▼

*Jesus, You in me,
it changes everything. Amen.*

▶ taking inventory:

WITH

1. It's been said that one overarching theme of the Bible is that no matter what people do, God is with us. In what moments in your life have you most clearly felt His presence with you?

2. How did focusing on the word *with* help you transform the lives of those you love?

3. Is there a certain thing you did to help you remember that God is with you amid uncertainty?

FAMILY

1. When you focused on the word *family*, did you find you were excluding people who do not fit with your "type" or "style" out of fear?

2. Did you reach out to anyone, letting them know they belong?

3. Have you ever struggled to feel as though you are part of God's family? Do you now know that you belong to Him?

WAIT

1. When is a specific time you had to wait on God? What was the outcome?

2. Why do you think God wants us to wait on Him instead of immediately answering our prayers, questions, or concerns?

3. How did you strengthen your resolve and trust Jesus at work?

JESUS

1. Scripture says that you "will receive power when the Holy Spirit has come upon you, and you will be my witnesses . . ." Did you use that power last week?

2. Does your life look as though you have been with Jesus?

3. If others surveyed your words and actions, would it help them understand more about the character of Jesus?

Dear Jesus, thank You that there is nowhere I go that You are not present. Give me courage and peace as I step forward, holding Your hand and trusting Your heart. You are always with me. Please continue to show me what it means to love like our Father. Help me be inclusive and generous, never letting my comfort zone determine my reach. Jesus, thank You for never letting my preferences determine Your plan. You are always on time and Your ways are perfect. Help me trust that. Show me how to wait in wisdom and in grace. I cannot count the many ways You've radically changed my life. Help me truly believe in You and help me to stand firm, boldly searching for opportunities to tap into Your extraordinary power in Me. You are the game-changer. In Jesus' name, amen.

Find these beautiful books and more on dayspring.com and at several retail stores near you.

ABOUT THE AUTHOR

CLEERE CHERRY REAVES is the owner and creator of Cleerely Stated, a successful business that started with a simple blog and turned into a full-blown gift line that can be found online and in retail stores. Well-known for her easy-to-relate, practical writing style, Cleere's passion is to help people recalibrate, refocus and remember who they are in Jesus. She was born and raised in Greenville, North Carolina. She's a proud Tarheel and a very happy newlywed.

Dear Friend,

This book was prayerfully crafted with you, the reader, in mind—every word, every sentence, every page—was thoughtfully written, designed, and packaged to encourage you...right where you are this very moment. At DaySpring, our vision is to see every person experience the life-changing message of God's love. So, as we worked through rough drafts, design changes, edits and details, we prayed for you to deeply experience His unfailing love, indescribable peace, and pure joy. It is our sincere hope that through these Truth-filled pages your heart will be blessed, knowing that God cares about you—your desires and disappointments, your challenges and dreams.

He knows. He cares. He loves you unconditionally.

BLESSINGS!
THE DAYSPRING BOOK TEAM

Additional copies of this book and other DaySpring titles can be purchased at fine retailers everywhere.
Order online at dayspring.com
or
by phone at 1-877-751-4347